David's People

Christina Stern

authorHOUSE®

AuthorHouse™ UK
1663 Liberty Drive
Bloomington, IN 47403 USA
www.authorhouse.co.uk
Phone: 0800.197.4150

Published by AuthorHouse 07/08/2016

ISBN: 978-1-5049-9914-4 (sc)
ISBN: 978-1-5049-9913-7 (e)

Print information available on the last page.

This book is printed on acid-free paper.

For Klara who I never knew,

And for David who I know so well!

Contents

Contents

ACKNOWLEDGEMENTS

With grateful thanks to my two good friends, Karen and Irene, only they know what for. Many thanks also to Jurgen Rundsheimer (now deceased) without him this book would not have been possible. And of course to my husband David who has suffered alongside me.

Timeline

In 1907, Simon died aged 74 leaving Jettchen his wife, a widow. This was a good age at that time and he had been a doting Grandfather of Selma (5), Karl (3) and Klara who was 2 at the time when Siegfried was born. In 1909, Siegfried died, possibly of Diphtheria. Remember, he was 41 when he married in 1874. In 1911, daughter Lina was alive and still living with her mother Jettchen. Jettchen died in 1912 at the grand age of 72. Adolph and Sarah were aged 39 and their children Selma, Karl and Klara were 10, 8 and 7 respectively. Dora had been born a year earlier.

1933	Adolph 60	Sarah 60	Selma 31	Karl 29	Klara 28	Dora 22
1934						
1935						To Frankfurt in June
1936						
1937						To Altenkirchen
1938				To Frankfurt	May – to Frankfurt	Returned to Frankfurt then Gladenbach
1938	KRISTALLNACHT ON NOVEMBER 11TH EVERYWHERE Klara went to England in December on a Kindertransport boat					
1939			In Frankfurt	Signed papers to be known as Isreal	In Harrogate until just before David was born	Signed papers to be known as Sarah
1940	Adolph and Sarah were 67 and the last Jews in Gladenbach. Karl started his journey to America and Klara was transported to the Isle of Man as an alien.					
1941	Adolph and Sarah made to wear Jewish Yellow Star sewn on their clothes.					
1942	Both sent to Terezin Sarah died 16th Sept Age 69		Sent East	In Chicago	David sent back to England from IOM Klara age 37	In Dominican Republic
1943	Adolph died 4th December Age 70			In Chicago	Klara released from IOM	In Dominican Republic
1944			23.8.to Stutthof Died 21.12 No. 70550 Age 42	Chicago		Chicago
1945				Seattle		Seattle
1946					Disappeared without trace. Age 41	
1950	David legally adopted.					

Who is David? - 1973

I met David on a Tuesday night. To be more precise it was Tuesday, 10th January 1973. Seems such a long time ago now and yet every detail is clear. Tuesday was girls' night out. There were four of us. All too young and attractive, all married, all of us had little kids, very little money, a tarnished view of love, partnership and parenting and a desperate need to reassure ourselves that there was life beyond wet nappies, chocolate buttons and 'The Wheels on the Bus'!

Tuesday night was free entry before 10 p.m. at the 'Poco a Poco' Night Club for us girls. In 1973 we weren't called women. Each week there was a different 'turn' on. Mostly struggling pop groups and has-been solo singers but it was better than staying at home. Armpits and legs shaved, hair washed, hot pants suits and make-up donned, we were ready for anything. Although it is true to say not one of us was daring enough to be looking for an extra-marital relationship to relieve the day to day boredom we were engulfed in. That is to say, we weren't consciously on the pull. Too scared! We just wanted some light relief and fun. We always set out together, sat together and went home together in my tin can of a car I had only just learned to drive. As it turned out, Tuesday 10th January 1973 was different. Two of the girls had cried off due to sick kids and taciturn husbands. That left only Irene and me. We decided to go any way, as there was a 'turn' on we both wanted to see. What a life changing night it turned out to be!

"Don't look now Irene, but there's a bloke over there holding a pint and leaning with his back to the bar watching us. He's been staring over for the past ten minutes. I wish he would either, come over and talk to us or clear off." Irene's back was to the bar so she couldn't see or feel him staring at us, but I could, even through the thick miasmic haze of cigarette smoke and dim night-club lights. Not bad! Not particularly tall but definitely dark, handsome and foreign looking. Hairy too! "Oh, oh, here he comes, get ready for the chat up line." His approach was purposeful but guarded. It was almost as though he was preparing himself for rejection. I looked at him closely and saw a gentle man who definitely did not exude confidence but did carry with him a real deep level of understanding and kindness in his soft hazel eyes. Here was a man who wanted and needed to be loved.

Even though I had recognised this in a fleeting instant, my first thought was, how unusual he has hazel eyes and is so dark skinned.

To both of us he said, "Hello, I'm David and I'm Jewish." I replied, 'Yes, and ....?'

It was the only reply I could think of at the time. Irene said nothing. Looking straight at me he said, "Would you like to dance?" I got up and we headed for the dance floor and from there on we never seemed to stop talking. We talked about the obvious. How often do you come here? What do think of this club? What do you do for a living? Are you married? Have you got children? Conversation was easy and we both behaved as if we had known each other all our lives. At the time I was a social worker, and so had an uncommon interest in other people's lives and what made them tick. With hindsight, maybe I was just plain nosey too. But I had an overwhelming need to reaffirm my own self. My past, my present and my future and most of all, my family roots. Marriage to the wrong person at a very young age had done nothing to support my past or make what I knew, concrete.

"David, why did you feel it was important for me to know you were Jewish?" The visible armour against rejection came back. It was so evident and strong I felt I could almost touch it. "Well, I know I'm Jewish, but I was adopted so don't ask me anything about me or my family because I don't know. All I do know is I've always been made to feel I'm different, even though I was adopted by a Jewish family. I can't claim to have been desperately ill-treated but I do know they adopted me for the wrong reasons and I do know I was always an outsider. I was eight years old when I was adopted into a comfortable family that already had one son older than me and a daughter who was younger. I always knew I was adopted and so I felt different. So since I grew up I've made a life for myself and put it all behind me. Where's the point in dwelling on the past?"

My own sense of family and family history had always been strong. I was fortunate to have had grandparents who told me fascinating stories about their lives and times. I had revelled in the love of an exceptional mother and I knew who I was. I could see the pain in David's eyes and asked, "Have you never wondered who your mother was and how you came to be adopted?" "Occasionally," he said. I found this very hard to accept, because I'd experienced the security of grandparents and a mother who had happily shared so many treasured stories and facts. I could look at so many family photographs and see who I looked like, knowing why I existed, why I had my characteristics, thoughts, interests and aspirations. I truly believed I knew who I was. But who was David? So I asked, "Do you have any memories at all about your past, your mother, who you are?"

It's a wonder he didn't excuse himself and offload me there and then! But true to his nature, (which I was to discover later), he humoured me. "I have only three clear childhood memories before I was adopted. I know my real surname is Stern. I remember the sound of warning sirens and someone carrying me, running, to an air-raid shelter and I remember living in a children's home. It was a day when I had been naughty and I was made to climb up a ladder into a dark loft and the trap door was closed on me. Other than that, I can't remember anything."

On January 8th 1977, I married David Stern. We had lived together since July 1973. My boys were ten and twelve by the time we got married and seemed to accept David well. My boys are now grown up and are fathers themselves, and I've been married to David for almost forty years. It certainly doesn't feel like it, and I continue to love him more every year that goes by. I really appreciate his goodness and kindness, and friends who have known him for many years are convinced he has a 'portrait in the attic', like Dorian Grey in the eponymous novel written by Oscar Wilde, as he does not seem to age. He's 76 now and just as handsome! With all its ups and downs, this is a record of what happened to other members of David's family.

Visit to Seattle - 1994

Today was going to be a life changing experience, I knew. As the Victoria Clipper neared Pier 70, its destination, David disappeared. I knew exactly where he would be - out on the top deck, desperately trying to get his first view of the family he had never met, without being seen. I was undecided whether to push my way through the crowds of people getting ready to disembark and join him up there, or to stay put and allow him the space he needed. As the Clipper edged into the dock, my indecision was interrupted by a vision through the lower deck windows - a vision I had conjured up in my mind many times throughout the years. Someone who David belonged to, and who belonged to him! There she was, Dora, his mother's sister. A tiny, white haired figure, frantically waving. She had seen him! It had been a long wait, fifty-five years in all and he deserved this moment to himself.

Tears flooded my eyes, my heart began to race, and my legs turned to jelly. So many emotions were fighting each other, I didn't know what to feel. Only his God knew what David was experiencing up there, alone on deck. I couldn't begin to imagine what it was like for him, and I still haven't dared to ask him to try to put it into words. Maybe I never will. It is perhaps one of those things that belongs only to him. After all, we should all be allowed to keep something special for ourselves and never have to share it.

Walking off the boat, along the gangway onto the Pier, through three sets of swing doors and into the meeting hall, felt like the longest journey we had ever made together. After the fierce bright sunshine, the hall seemed dark and gloomy and it was difficult to see, especially as there were so many people milling around. Suddenly it was as if everyone else melted into the background. Dora, silhouetted in the gloom against the sunlight streaming in through glass doors, clapped her hands with joy and came towards David with open arms. They clung to each other for the longest time, each one in turn trying to let go and not wanting to. I tried my best to capture the moment on video film, but my hands were shaking so much and the light was so poor, the end result would not by any stretch of the imagination win a prize.

I eventually got to hug this precious little woman, whilst David greeted her chaperones, his cousin Sara, and her husband Harry, pronounced by Sara in a strong American accent, and grating voice. Both of them must have weighed in at 280lbs plus, and as we were to learn later, they epitomised everything that is negative about American stereotypes.

Out into the sunshine and a brief walk along the waterfront, then we all piled into the biggest station wagon I have ever seen. Dora continued to hug and touch David, whilst her husband turned the ignition key several times. Nothing! Not a peep! Ah well, welcome to Seattle! By this time, Sara was getting redder and redder in the face and I couldn't work out if it was due to the heat, her weight, embarrassment, anger, or a mixture of all. Or simply the fact that, as we discovered later, she was a rather egotistical, immature fifty year old, who couldn't cope with any disruption in her life in any way, shape or form. By this time, I was feeling slightly hysterical and could only see the funny side. David started laughing too, but the American contingency was not amused!

Every suggestion Dora made they told her to shut up, even when she was offering to pay for a tow, a repair, or a taxi. Eventually, we got a taxi and David paid $30. It emerged later that Dora had given Sara the money for a taxi, and also $100 to have the car towed to the garage. The tow, by the way, only cost $70, but no change was ever forthcoming. Dora also gave them some money to pay for the repairs. This was to be the pattern of the rest of our stay.

As we had left Nanaimo during the morning to get to Victoria, by the time we boarded the Clipper boat at 2pm, we were both hungry. We decided to treat ourselves to a little luxury and have bagels, cream cheese and smoked salmon (Jewish people call smoked salmon 'lox'). It was absolutely wonderful, and so filling I purposely left some, as I thought Dora was bound to have a meal ready in advance for us. It was now well past 6pm, and the journey in the taxi had taken almost twenty five minutes. As we neared Dora's house, she looked at us lovingly, and in her broken English and strong German accent said, "You are hungry-yes? I haf a surprise for you. I haf lox and bagels and cream cheese. You eat it-yes? You like it-yes?" Welcome to Seattle!

Dora has a lovely, spacious four bed roomed house with a large, pretty garden. Dora's daughter and her husband live next door to her, although she hardly sees them. On arrival, she immediately showed us to a room she had prepared for us, and instructed us to treat it, and the rest of the house, as our own. We were to do anything we wanted to do, and to ask for anything at all and it would be granted. We should also give her our laundry when we had any. Needless to say we didn't! She said emphatically (and continued to say it again and again throughout the time we were there) that we belonged to her, and anything she had belonged to us. Sara and her husband, as well as the other 'delightful' family members whom I shall describe anon, all clearly took her at her word. Sara and Harry stayed for the meal, and Dora's grandson and granddaughter also turned up to eat. Dora clearly had expectations that we would eat vast amounts of food, as she'd bought enough lox and bagels to feed about twenty people. God knows what it had cost, but Sara and her husband et al, did their best to clear it. It even defeated them! Meal over, they all went home and left the washing up. This, we learned, was usual behaviour, and when David started to wash up, Dora was totally bemused.

I had quickly realized that within this group, nobody smoked or drank alcohol, so I spent the rest of the time sneaking outside for a cigarette and inevitably, someone would unfailingly follow me out to talk to me. I never had a smoke in peace. Thank God we had a bottle of booze stashed away in the bedroom cupboard, where we were reduced to one secret drink before going to sleep at night. After our liquid week in Nanaimo, we were beginning to suffer withdrawal symptoms.

The week went by in a stressful haze, but before I tell you about some of the happenings, it's maybe a good idea if I describe all the characters, so that you can get a real feel for the 'Seattle Experience.' After spending a full week with them all, I felt so angry by the time I got home to England, I couldn't wait for the cathartic experience of writing down my feelings and recording the details of it all. It is for this reason that the following part is particularly subjective!

Dora

In a nutshell, Dora is the sweetest person anyone could ever meet. Tiny and at 82 (nearly 83) she is one amazing lady. The stories she told me about her survival in Germany, and then later in America, were incredible. All will be revealed in this, my blockbuster first novel - they'll be clamouring for the film rights, I think. She speaks with a very heavy German accent, and frequently joins her German and English words together. She is soft and gentle, and wants to hug and touch constantly. A hundred times she said to David, "I luff you so much sweedheart, everything I haff is yours, you don't know how much this means to me, just ask me for anything - you can haff it, pleases come again, I cry when you go, I vill send you the money!"

She keeps the house and garden like a new pin, does all her own washing and ironing, walks two blocks for her shopping and carries it back, constantly cooks wonderful meals, and asks if you are you hungry about every hour. Her fridge overflows with food, and as soon as there is a little bit of space on a shelf, she goes shopping again. This year she painted the whole of her garden herself, which seems to go on for miles. Mind you, when you get to know and understand her wonderful family, you begin to realise that she has no choice. It seems that the only function she serves is to keep bailing her family members out of their money troubles. She pays both daughters' house taxes, buys their cars, and anything else they seem to be able to persuade her into acquiring. She even has to pay someone to cut her grass and carry in the wood from the woodpile in the winter. But down at the shopping mall, everyone knows and loves her. The staff in all of the shops she went in treated her with the greatest respect - shame her family don't seem do the same.

Dora's daughter - Sara

Sara lives next door to her mother, and rarely shows her face to Dora unless she wants some money or food! She is a shopaholic, who surrounds herself with the most expensive, garish possessions. Her house resembles that of a Romany Gypsy, all cut glass, colourful but expensive ornaments, and loud colours; however, the garden resembles a rubbish dump. She never cooks a meal, she says that she hates her kids, and according to her, that they hate her too. When out shopping, she makes statements such as, "If I see it, I godda buy it, just can't live withoud it, I really neeeed it!" She then flies into a tantrum if someone buys 'it' before her - we experienced this one day on the market in downtown Seattle.

On the surface, she pretended to make a big fuss of David and me, but it was clear that she felt threatened by this new arrival (David), who may just muscle in on her inheritance. It was becoming clear that there was a sense of Sara almost looking forward to her mother's death. Dora told me that Sara had even asked her how much she would get in the Will, at which point Sara apparently plans to go to Hawaii, in style! Sara went as far as to tell myself and David a very tasteless joke about the subject, thinking it was very funny. Then, she stated how much she loved her mother, and how *we* shouldn't upset her. She gave me a lecture about how lonely and unwell her mother was, and how much damage our visit could do to her.

Sara works for an Insurance firm, earns reasonable money and lives from pay cheque to pay cheque. She seemed extremely jealous of her sister, as if she couldn't bear the thought that her sister may get more from her mother than she does. Get the picture?

Harry - Sara's husband

Harry is a stereotypical, overweight American, who does absolutely as little as possible whilst at home. He usually dresses in a vest and shorts, and eats at least three helpings of whatever is on offer. He works in a bakery and gets home around two in the afternoon. Harry spends the rest of his time eating and watching old movies on video. He has a collection of 700 films, and adds to them on a regular weekly basis. Harry does, however, cook occasionally, but is more inclined to see what Dora has in her kitchen, where he then eats, and goes home. He obviously has no qualms about accepting money from Dora, as he happily sat back and let her pay for everyone whenever we were all out together.

Dora's Grandson - Simon (Sara and Harry's son, aged 24)

Simon is a good looking, very intense young man, with a recent history that nobody talks about. Apparently, he was in the Marines for a while, but we never discovered what happened. He's lived with his grandmother, Dora, for two years and pretty well ignores his parents. He earns his living as a landscape gardener, and has an obsession with tracing his roots and Family Tree. He had decided, for some unknown reason, to change his surname from Brown to Browne, presumably because he has never felt he belonged with his parents? He was, by all accounts very close to his grandfather Ernst (Dora's husband), who had died six years previously. I couldn't make my mind up about his relationship with Dora, as he professed to love her, but apparently (according to Dora), flew into uncontrollable rages, making her very afraid of him. He never pays her a penny for living there, and she does everything for him, including feeding him and his girlfriend, who is always present. Considering that Dora has to pay someone to cut the grass and bring in wood, you can maybe work out just how much he cares.

Dora's grand-daughter – Sarah (Sara and Harry's daughter, aged 22)

Sarah is very pretty, but has a haunted look about her. She says that she hates her parents, was married at seventeen (Dora told me she paid for the wedding), and had a baby. Her son, (who was the same age as our grandson), lived with her husband's mother and father who, we were told, were alcoholics. Sarah had separated, and was seeing a therapist due to having developed an eating disorder. She was living with a drug- using boyfriend, and although she was alone with me for only fifteen minutes, seemed to see me as a free therapist, spilling out her life story. She told me that she had been sexually abused between the ages of nine and twelve years old, and that when she had 'spilled the beans' at fifteen years old, she was glad and relieved when everyone had believed her.

It was apparent that Dora worries so much about her great-grandson (Sarah's child) and the kind of upbringing he is getting, that she regularly gives Sarah money to buy some clothes and shoes for him. Sarah frequently drops in on Dora to see what she can eat or scrounge. Despite this, Dora really worries about her, loves her for all her faults, and has offered to pay for her through College if only she will try to make something of her life. Sarah has never held down a job. We got the impression that she was waiting for Dora's grandson to move out (he's supposed to be going to share an apartment with his girlfriend), and then she intended to move in with grandma. She told me, "Grandma is the only one who never lets me down." I wondered if she had also said that to Dora, piling on the guilt and making sure that she always had a bolt hole?

Mona - (the youngest daughter, who lives a five minute car drive away).

Mona is exactly the same age as me. She is big and overweight, with dyed black hair. She wears a lot of T-shirts, and suits with gold motifs, and lots of jewellery. She has a mania for crystal ornaments, blob lamps, and does most of her shopping via the TV shopping channel QVC, using Dora's credit card. She has hundreds of pairs of shoes, and four wardrobes full of clothes. The house is relatively small, and crammed with 'stuff'. There are several fibre optic, multi-coloured lamps and loud, Blackpool- type mementoes and plastic flowers.

Mona has a good job in a bank, with her own secretary and office. I think she must earn pretty big bucks. She met her husband when she was fifteen, and they finally married thirteen years later. She stayed at home with her parents for all of those years, likewise her husband. They have no children, and a week before we arrived, she had undergone a hysterectomy for health reasons.

Just like Sara, Mona has a grating voice, and by the end of our time there, I had had enough of hearing about the operation, about how many pain pills she had to take and how they made her feel, how good her husband was, and how much she loved her mother.

Mona would arrange outings to the most expensive restaurants, and then let Dora pay. At least she does go to see her mother regularly, but I suspect it might be to collect anything that she thinks might be due to her. She calls Dora "Maarmaa," and is very subtle at getting money out of her. Mona's most recent triumph was an expensive car!

Mona pretended to understand and enjoy David's sense of humour, but in reality, it seemed to go over her head, or leave her feeling threatened, I think. She never cooked a meal either, but when I tell you about her husband, perhaps you will understand why.

Leroy - (Mona's husband)

Not a lot to say about Leroy, except that he seems very lazy, and I found him rather odd. In fact, their marriage seems very odd. Each panders to the other, calling each other honey and sweetie, in a child-like manner. Leroy decided, eleven years ago, to stop working. As far as David and I could make out, there was absolutely nothing wrong with him, except that they both kept telling us about his high cholesterol count. (Strikes me that America is cholesterol mad!) Probably due to all the junk food they eat. The most energetic thing Leroy seemed to do was a bit of vacuuming, some cooking, and restoring an old Cadillac that belonged to Ernst. Dora also gave him a very fancy station wagon which used to belong to her husband.

So Leroy appeared to be quite happy with the arrangement of Dora paying most of their overheads, in return for showing minimal interest in her life.

Getty - (now deceased, and widow of Karl)

Getty is (was) the wife of Karl, who died in 1982; this made her David's aunt, and his mother's and Dora's sister-in-law. David has christened her 'Getty the Witch'. She is a perfect stereotype - a loud, know-all immigrant. She is an ageing Jewess, with an American/German accent, who is money wise, and someone who has 'made it'. That is to say, Karl made it. She is everyone's idea of a typical, rich, American Jewish widow. She, I think, was the most threatened by David's appearance out of the woodwork, and it is no wonder.

Dora told us that unknown to her, Klara, David's mother, during her early years in England, and must have had an address for Karl in America, as she wrote several pleading letters to Karl, asking him to send her money so that she could go to the States. He had made it to America during the war, and had succeeded in making a lot of money. He was a trained 'bespoke tailor' and made officers' uniforms. He had set up a very lucrative business in Seattle, offering high class tailoring, dry cleaning and an invisible repairs service. It seems he got a lot of contract work from the Services, and was also engaged in a black market run to Canada, buying up exclusive English worsted materials that were in demand, and almost like gold then. But he refused to send any money to Klara, saying that he was ashamed of her because she had a baby but was not married.

Jewish religious beliefs and traditions dictate that sex outside marriage is a very great sin. It was almost as bad as marrying out of the faith, and as you probably know, when that person was declared dead, a Kaddish was said and no one ever mentioned his or her name again. The awful irony is that when he married Getty, she was already pregnant with her son, about whom you will learn more later. They told everyone that Getty's son was Karl's. By now you will realise that David is the only male left of the Stern family, who could legally and rightfully carry on the name. It's only in recent years that the truth has come out.

Getty ruled Karl and the marriage with an iron fist, and she was not prepared to share anything they had with anyone. The result was that she convinced Karl not to help Klara, and to keep it secret from Dora. According to Dora, it seems that Klara must have scraped the money together to advertise in Aufbau, in search of Dora. This is the German/Jewish newspaper which is circulated all over the world, and which, for decades, Jews have used to trace their loved ones. Believe it or not, I advertised in exactly the same newspaper five years ago, to see if I could trace anyone in the States belonging to David. As an aside, many years before, I had been told by a spiritualist medium that there was someone in America who wanted to meet David. I got the same result as Klara - nothing.

The saddest part is that Karl saw the advert, and Dora didn't. He never told her until years afterwards, when he produced it and tore it up in front of her. As you can imagine, she has many bitter feelings. Poor Dora carries massive guilt about this, but how could she do anything when she didn't know! She confided that she has spent many days and nights crying over this, and worrying and wondering what happened to her beloved sister. From what Dora says, she, Selma (the sister who went to the concentration camp) and Klara were all really close.

Mine and David's rationalisation at this point was that maybe there was a 'master plan', because if things had been different, we would never have met. Anyway, Getty told us a cock- and- bull story of how Karl had sent Klara money, but that Klara had been mentally ill. We know different, as I have all the original case notes that tell of her abject poverty and total powerlessness in her circumstances. Also, prior to our arrival, Getty had told Dora that the letters from Klara still existed, but when we had asked for them, she said that they had been destroyed as she had moved so many times since Karl died. She was very cagey about everything, so we gave it up as a bad job.

I think also that she was panicking, in case the truth came out, and David may lay claim to anything that she saw as rightfully hers. She showed us a photograph of Karl as a young man, and it was like looking at David's face. Sara, also, had said that David reminded her of Uncle Karl, especially when he laughed. She said it was an identical sound.

Getty's Son - Stan

There's not a lot to say about Stan, except that he is an amiable, fairly likeable wastrel who loves travelling the world, and makes a living where he can. He had one unsuccessful marriage many years ago, and now lives alone in what amounts to a mansion. At present, he's a professional poker play and earns amazing amounts. He's determined to do more travelling, and be able to stay wherever he wants, for as long as he wants. When I suggested this would take a lot of money, with a wicked grin he pointed out that's just what he would have when his mother died.

By now, you will realise that David is the only male left of the Stern family, who could legally and rightfully carry on the name. It's only in recent years that the truth has come out.

I have already described our first Saturday with David's family members. I will now tell you about what happened during the rest of our week's stay at Dora's, in the form of an abbreviated diary.

Sunday

The weather was hot, and we sat in the garden a lot. David has a leisurely breakfast of lox, pickled cucumbers, pickles herring and black bread, with Dora. I felt sick just watching! Then Dora's eldest daughter and her best friend insist that they take us to a Street Craft Fair in a neighbouring town. This was because *they* wanted to go. The temperature was around 95F and not really the weather for walking around. On arrival, Dora's eldest daughter and her friend took off at ten miles an hour, totally disregarding Dora's needs. We caught them up and told them to go it alone, and to meet us later. We met up later when Dora's daughter was hungry. We went to a place of her choosing, ate, andthen Dora paid for everyone. More walking, now it felt like a 100 degrees and no concern for Dora. They went off again and we sat in the shade with Dora for two hours. When we returned home, everyone descended for the evening meal (including the grandchildren, younger sister and her husband, Getty and son) and then they all left after they'd eaten all the food, leaving all the washing up.

Monday

Dora's grandson, Simon, was on a day off from work, and suggested we all go out for breakfast. Nice, I thought. But all the gang came too, Sara complaining because she couldn't choose where to go. And Dora paid! Later we went round the shopping malls, and when we returned home, Dora cooked. All descended to eat, and then left.

Tuesday

Harry was on his weekly day off. Me, David, Dora, Sara and Harry go to downtown Seattle and the big waterfront market. Sara plus husband, walk at ten miles an hour again, with no consideration for Dora. We look after her, but feel it is much too much for someone of 82, what with the crowds and the heat. Into a nice restaurant, of Sara's choosing, and this time David pays for everyone. We endured more looking round shops, back to the car, stop, and even more looking round shops. All this of Sara's choosing, I might add. On Sara's instructions, we stop at an ice-cream parlour with thirty-one different flavours. She and David go in. I follow to make sure Dora gets what she wants. We get served and Sara offers to pay for her own - not anyone else's I might add. I was so disgusted I just said to David "You pay eh!" The day had been so long, their voices so annoying and the weather so hot that by this time Dora was nearly dead, and David was ready to tell Sara a few home truths. Only with my gentle persuasion did he keep his mouth shut.

Wednesday

Dora insisted that David went flying, (having successfully acquired a Private Pilot's Licence some years earlier), and that she paid. This was getting embarrassing but after some heart searching it clearly meant so much to her that he agreed. He visited the Boeing Factory and flew over all of Seattle and the Islands and Dora and I at last got a quiet day to really talk. I was able to share everything I had discovered with her and she shared a lot of history with me.

In the early evening an arrangement has been made to go to Mona's for dinner, but we then discover she and her husband are picking us up, and we are actually going out to dinner somewhere quite expensive and then on to their house. I can't remember what we did in the day - it was that interesting! We were picked up at 5.00pm to go to the restaurant. Main courses were expensive and Mona very subtly tries to make believe they are treating us and paying, but guess who pays! In no time at all, we then travel to their house and the coloured fibre optic lamps. I remember thinking at least they drink, and Leroy used to smoke until not long ago, so it's not too bad except for the stories of the operation and the pain pills!

Thursday

We went to the shops in the morning, and there was a summons to attend Getty at her apartment on Capitol Hill at three in the afternoon. There was also an arrangement to be picked up by Mona and her husband at five thirty to go and visit his parents for the evening. Getty was hyper and had made mountains of food. Strudel and other special cake were the order of the day and, on our arrival and regardless of the fact that Dora had got the dinner in the oven, she forced us to stay for dinner. Mountains of cold cuts, salads, pickles, cake and so on. After calling Mona's house to say that we would be late, we then went on to Leroy's parents for more food, alcohol, and a show by their singing parrot.

Friday

This was our one and only day where we had a little bit of time to ourselves. We had to fight for it mind you. We went on the bus, back to the waterfront market and wandered to our hearts content. Returned to a lovely dinner cooked by Dora. That was after having to spell out to Sara that she would have to cancel a booking she had made at an ultra expensive Japanese restaurant for all of us. This was without consulting us! Guess who would have had to pay?

Saturday

We had some more of Sara, her husband and best friend. They had booked us all out on a trip to a neighbouring island that was a Native Indian Reservation. This was especially designed for tourists at a cost of $38 each for 4 hours. We did get a lunch of fresh salmon and salad and North West Indian Dances thrown in, as well as being ripped off. Ah well, it was one for the photograph album. On arrival back in Seattle, we had more walking round the famous market........

Early evening Getty and son appear again. Dora and Getty still clearly dislike each other.

Another stressful encounter!

Ancestors - Christian or Jew?

This theme seems to have run through the family throughout time, as you will see. What difference does it make in the end? We are all, or have been, people who have lived, loved, suffered losses and made gains throughout our lives. We are a collection of human beings, who have failings and strengths, hopes and dreams and who do our best at the time. We keep our fingers crossed and hope that our best was good enough. Who knows, maybe it was and maybe it wasn't.

The story begins in the middle of the Eighteenth Century - that is around 1775, in the country we now know today as Germany. In those days, Germany did not exist as it does now. It was divided into many smaller 'countries' and what were then called Principalities. The place was a very small village called Gladenbach in Germany, a beautiful place, nestling amongst hills and dales. The nearest very big cities were/and still are, Kassel in the North, and Frankfurt in the South. Gladenbach is only a few kilometres from Marburg, which has one of the oldest Universities in Germany. The University was established well before 1775, and in fact the Brothers Grimm (who wrote all the fairy tales) studied there in 1802-5. So you can see, they were contemporaries of Wolf Stern, (David's great-great-great-grandfather), and he may have even met them! Marburg and Gladenbach were very pretty places; all the houses were black and white and quite 'higgledy piggledy'. The streets were lined with trees (they still are today) and looked just like many of the illustrations in the Grimm Brothers fairy tales. The surrounding countryside was mainly beautiful forests and hills.

Photo of Houses in Marburg

Wolf lived in Gladenbach at this time. It has not been possible to find his date of birth, but there is a record in existence that in 1775, he was already adult and had been accepted onto the Register of Jewish Patrons. I think it is probably safe to assume that he was born somewhere around 1750. In 1777 he was listed as having a property in Gladenbach consisting of a house and stabling. Its insurable value was 800 Guilders, so he must have been quite a rich and important man. Wolf was originally called Wolf Liebmann (which meant Wolf, son of Lieb). On 3rd of March 1809, he changed his surname to Stern. He married a woman called Esther, but there is no record of the date. I don't know how many children he had, but two further references lead me to believe he that had more than one. Upon his death in 1830, if my calculations are correct, he would have been 80 years old. His children inherited his house, and David's great-great-grandfather, Abraham, was referred to as Wolf's youngest son.

Abraham was born on 2nd July 1789, and if, for instance, Wolf married when he was in his late twenties, this would fit with the fact that Jews had to obtain permission to marry, and were often only granted this permission over the age of twenty five, this being a deliberate strategy to keep the Jewish population down. He could have been married between ten and fourteen years before Abraham was born. Wolf was certainly approaching forty when his youngest son came into the world so there could have been quite a lot of children.

To begin to understand what life must have been like for Wolf and his family in those times, and why he decided to change his name when he was in his fifties, (history does repeat itself as you will see later), you need to be able to get a feel for the general atmosphere in Germany then. The Laws governed how Jewish communities lived, and what attitudes and prejudices they were faced with! My apologies in advance for the ensuing history lesson.

From 1760 onwards was a time of great change in Germany. It was known as the period of 'Enlightenment and Emancipation'. Prior to this time, Jews had been regarded as no more than a part of a dispersed nation. This meant they were seen wholly as Jews, and not as German citizens or subjects. The most conspicuous Jewish communities in Europe lived in Germany and Austria, approximately 175,000 in population by 1800. That is roughly one Jew to every hundred Germans in those days, the biggest majority being 'Ashkenazi,' the 'common type,' who had originated from the Middle East and Spain in the Middle Ages and later from Russia and Poland.

Jews lived very separate lives from others, often by their own choice, and only mixed to do business. Family life, education, adult study and religious services were exclusive to them. Jewish society was regarded by everyone as traditional. All culture, values and religion (it's very mainstay) were seen as being derived from the past. In fact, Jews were seen as having a total reliance on the past.

Jews did not see themselves as belonging to the place where they lived; this was only a temporary abode amongst other nations. This must have re-affirmed everybody else's view of them. Christian society stereotyped Jews, hence the prejudices. Orthodox Ashkenazi Jews were conspicuous by their appearance. Their strange clothes - men wore long black coats and wide brimmed hats, which made them stand out amongst the fashions of the day. The men also favoured curly side locks and long beards; the women were quietly dressed in dark colours and once married, wore wigs. This was a custom so that no man other than their husband would ever see their 'crowning glory', their hair! Orthodox Jews still dress like this, even in today's society.

The language they spoke was a mixture of German and Hebrew, which later became known as Yiddish. At that time in Germany, there was a great swing towards people speaking what is known as 'High German'. A bit like us saying someone speaks 'the Queen's English'. Anyone who didn't speak this was looked upon as uneducated. Even if a Jew spoke High German, it was often with a Yiddish accent, and was regarded as a laughable jargon. Add to this all of the other prejudices, and you can begin to see that language delivery was easily attached to all other things Jewish that were despised.

Jewish communities paid towards the upkeep of their own synagogues, schools, 'Yeshivot' (schools for higher Talmudic learning), societies for caring for the sick and especially, the 'burial society'. Their status was based on two things: - Wealth and Talmudic learning. Wealth and learning supported each other and helped the Jews climb up the social ladder. Marriages were often arranged with families who lived far apart. If a youth went to a 'Yeshiva' in a famous Jewish Community, it was seen as commendable. Family commitment, tradition and religion tied the individual. Jews were expected to form communities and control their own day-to-day issues i.e. marriage, although marriage needed special permission due to population policies, divorce, inheritance etc. Matters were usually dealt with according to Talmudic law. If not satisfied with the outcome, Jews could apply to 'other' courts.

Jews in villages and towns joined together to form 'Landgemeinde' (a word used to describe mediation powers). This organisation mediated between Jews and the existing powers. They collected the taxes and had some control over the Jewish population. The 'Landgemeinde' also employed a Rabbi to oversee the religious side of life.

The Rabbis were very powerful, they had freedom to decide punishments for the individual who had transgressed and sexual 'sins' were considered to be the gravest of all. I do hope Wolf never committed such a sin, as I dread to think of his punishment! As a result of belonging to this close knit Jewish community, well known, rich and powerful Jews were appointed to the Register of Jewish Patrons. I suppose this answers my question about Wolf's conduct, as surely he would never have been appointed if he were a philanderer. Or maybe he was just never found out! This was very typical of the area and atmosphere David's great-great-great grandfather Wolf lived in.

Jews did not live dispersed and divided, as they were not allowed to settle where they pleased. Permission to reside in any locality depended on the goodwill of the Local Authorities. Jews were seen as alien and could be expelled without violation of any law. Certain cities remained closed to Jews, such as Strasbourg, Colmar and Munster. In Nuremburg, Jews could only be there during the daytime, and then had to even be accompanied by a local inhabitant. A strict curfew meant that they had to leave the City walls by dusk. In the City of Leipzig, Jews had an important role to play in the great fairs, a regular feature and a source of great income for the city, but they were not welcome to live there. According to the Leipzig city records, in 1753 only two Jewish families lived in the whole of the city. However, Peddlers (schnorrers) and tinkers did visit Leipzig during daylight hours. Permission to live somewhere was granted in exchange for payment of special levies (taxes) and failure to pay taxes meant expulsion, the harshest of all punishments. Terms of residence also strictly limited fields of occupation. Only certain occupations were allowed. Some Jews were more privileged than others due to the acquisition of money.

I have come to kind of expect that Wolf belonged to this group; others had no rights of residence. 'Right of residence' came with a job, for example, being a servant to another Jew. Others became wanderers and went from city to city, begging. They relied on other Jews for help but were disliked by all, including the rest of the Jewish population. Even the privileged Jews were still bound by rights of occupation. They were usually dealing in money lending or some type of trade. The Christians liked to think they were above this type of occupation and even went so far as to try and prove they were forbidden to deal in money by Christian teaching and Law.

Just as an aside, in 1812 there appeared the book 'Wider die Juden' (Grattenauer 1812) which carried the sub-title, 'A word of warning to all our Christian co-citizens.' The book tried to prove that Jews were permitted by their religion to cheat and rob Christians and to take false oath against them. The warning was all about preventing Christians agreeing to give 'citizenship' to the Jews. This was, of course, a very anti-Jewish attitude.

Due to the success of Jewish money deals, fears of their power grew in the Christian community. One clear statement that was made was, "for the greatest capital sums are in the hands of the Jews; for to the Jews all means are the same in order to attain their objective." (Burleigh 2000). Christians considered that Jews were ever present when a business opportunity was around. Any good Christian could fall easy prey to the cunning mind of a Jew. It was said, "It is mightily hard for the Jew to part with money - ready money is very dear to his heart." (Burleigh 2000)

A Jew who wished to be accepted in non-Jewish society had to dispel the notion of clinging to the idea of being a Jew, to prove by his behaviour that he was an exception.

Some other sayings of the day were, "Jews cling to too many superstitious opinions, to many useless and ridiculous customs, invented for expedience, by numerous Rabbis and that is the main reason for the isolated lives they live amongst us." (Burleigh 2000). Even if one found some Jews who had acquired 'Enlightenment', this did not necessarily make them more sociable. Some Jews stick selfishly to their own particular objectives; they despise other less educated and more indigent Jews while they themselves differ only outwardly from their despised fellow men. Mentally they are occupied with the same business matters - with bills of exchange, with pledges and mortgages and the interest to be collected in due course. There are, therefore, many reasons why Christians recoil from any kind of social intercourse with the 'Israelites'. There was also an overriding belief that Jews were dirty! I'm not sure where that idea came from.

For the less successful Jews, peddling trinkets, buying and selling clothing and cattle dealing were all recognised occupations. Jews, prior to this time, were not accepted in Universities, therefore it was almost impossible for them to become Doctors, Lawyers or any other member of a 'profession' that required any level of 'higher learning'. Neither were they allowed to engage in the making or selling of their own handicrafts of being joiners, builders, craftsmen, nor engage in agriculture. Strangely enough, though, they were allowed to become tailors and metalworkers. As a consequence there were no Jewish farmers! The petty trader or peddler (schnorrer) was the most despised of tradesmen, even though they travelled miles to cities, towns and villages and brought goods to the buyer's doorstep. Jews of this kind were seen as morally deficient and even corrupt.

A typical feature of working life was to have business connections in far-flung cities. Lots of travelling around was an accepted part of reality. Even the more humble retailers and peddler moved around neighbourhoods, travelling to wherever there was any promise of business. Outside contact was seen as a necessity to making a living. When you consider that travel was only either undertaken on foot or by horse, (if you were rich enough to hire or own one!), and the roads were probably pretty poor, this must have been a valuable service.

Great efforts were made by some to shed the more conspicuous features of Judaism. Perhaps at the time, 'Liebmann' was considered to be a typically Jewish name and 'Stern' (meaning star) was not. Who knows! Perhaps Wolf also adopted the fashions of the day in exchange for his long, black coat and wide brimmed hat. Maybe he even had his hair cut short.

In 1780, 'Emancipation' became the fashion. Several 'Edicts' and 'Laws' were passed during the following years, leading too much arguing as to whether Jews could or would ever be integrated. The first phase of Emancipation took a third of a century, that is to say that between the years of 1780-1814 many changes were to occur, but these changes happened very slowly. In 1780 Wolf would have been around thirty years old and I guess he was very politically aware when Emperor Joseph II of Austria passed the 'Edict of Tolerance Act' in 1781. Essentially, what the 'Act' said was that 'others' should be more tolerant of the Jews and they classed them as 'belonging' and of 'use' and welcomed them as 'citizens'.

The non-Jewish people were not happy with this; as far as they were concerned, the incompatibility of the Jewish religion and mentality, compared with the obligations of citizenship were the main argument. It was said that, Jews have traversed seventeen centuries and not mixed with other nations. Jews would not be able to serve in the army, nor do useful work in agriculture and industry. Their religion and their indolence would hinder them. The occupations the Jews excel in are finance and commerce and they do so at the expense of those who earned their bread by the sweat of their brow. Such were the attitudes and prejudice that all Jews were subjected to.

Arguments about Jews serving in the Army were based around the observation of the Sabbath, their laws and food. Such as, 'as long as Jews keep the Laws of Moses, as long as for instance they do not take their meals with us and, at mealtimes or over a simple glass of beer are unable to make friends, they will never fuse with us.' It was said that the dietary laws preclude fraternisation and intermingling: these same laws and observances of the Sabbath would hinder Jews from rendering the citizen's duty of protecting his country in times of war. For how can a Jew join the Army if he is unable to eat a soldier's food and feels religiously obliged to stop work on Saturdays? "Jews will never be able to regard the country in which they live to be more than a temporary abode, which they hope one day to leave and return to Israel, they will always be classed as the wandering Jew. A people that has such hopes, will never entirely feel at home or have patriotic love for the paternal soil."

I have a mental picture of Wolf as being a very astute, intelligent man who cared not only about his own family but also about his fellow men, rights of freedom and equality. I can just see him putting forward very lucid argument, cultivating non-Jewish powerful friends, who were themselves sympathetic to the plight of Jews. He had a dream and was prepared to do anything to see it come true! During those years many wars were fought in Germany and the surrounding countries. How frustrating it must have been to feel so powerless and not even be able to join the army and fight for what you believed in.

The granting of 'Citizenship in France for the Jews' by the National Assembly followed in the years of 1790-1. This helped the German Jews with their case. I bet Wolf was pleased! He would know that this must mean a better future for his children, especially his youngest and last - Abraham, who was now one year old.

Between the years 1791 and 1806 there was unrestricted freedom for Jewish people. They could even now join the army! This had never been experienced in the lifetimes of those living in Germany then. Some Jews left their former abodes and took advantage of the opportunity to go to other towns and cities where they had previously been forbidden to live. More Jews from the countryside moved to the towns. Clearly from the evidence, Wolf stayed put in his own village but I feel sure he would have travelled extensively. They were often away from home for weeks or months at a time.

Competition amongst trading Jews became severe. The Jewish answer to their business ventures and tactics was that all other avenues of fruitful endeavour were closed to them. There was what is known as a 'mobility collective' – when one moved, so did another. Change of residence sometimes also brought about a change of occupation. Some moved into agriculture, handicrafts and professions. Jews acquired landed property in Germany. Land was power. If borrowers failed to pay, the debtors land automatically fell into the hands of their Jewish lender. I believe that Wolf must have been quite a businessman to acquire so much wealth when he was relatively young. He probably struck deals with Christians, arranging mortgages on their properties. That way his customers would be indebted to him and would maybe help support his political fight.

During the years between 1808-13 in Frankfurt, well-to-do, middle class Jews used capital to do business with peasantry, providing loans, advancing money on crops, buying up and selling at a profit. Property and anything else that came along by chance, was regarded as a business venture. 'Usuary' (money-lending) was regarded by the rest of German society as taking advantage of the peasants' hard times, and the lower peddler business was regarded as obnoxious as it enticed the peasant to spend more than he had!

The Edict of 1809 determined the status of Jews in the country. It made the granting of communal and civil rights dependant on the individual Jew proving that he was engaged in 'an accepted occupation.' For instance the sedentary hawker, cattle dealer, moneylender or pawnbroker was refused this privilege. By 1809, Wolf would have been fifty-nine years old, and probably a well recognised and accepted member of the community in Gladenbach. I shouldn't think he had any difficulties in gaining his own 'civil rights'!

The Edict also established the 'Oberrat'. This was an organisation to direct young Jews into new occupations. Sums of up to 10,000 guilders had to be obtained from the community for training future artisans and agriculturalists. Maybe Wolf became a true philanthropist, helping those young people around him who wanted to develop their skills and knowledge and most of all, have their freedom. However, overall through these years, the occupational structure changed only marginally, and even up to a hundred years later, Jews were still only mainly operating within the recognised occupations. Maybe that had something to do with children inheriting family businesses.

The Edict of 1812 granted almost complete emancipation for the Jews. This was part of the general reform of the Prussian State following their defeat by Napoleon in 1806. You need to remember that the Napoleonic Wars were going on throughout many of these years, and also 1789 was the year of the French Revolution. There were many losses in battle and many Jewish soldiers died fighting for their homeland. Emancipation meant the State would now control everyone, not just Landgemeine. A law was passed that Jews must now begin to speak correct German and not Yiddish, in all matters pertaining to business, even if not at home. Wolf must have been furious at this infringement of civil liberties, but I dare guess he, personally, had learned to speak 'High German,' an aid to doing business many years before. This was seen as helping break down the barriers. Emancipation involved 'education', the new expectation being that Jews would learn the language (German), and they were encouraged to drop their own vernacular as it was regarded as crude and graceless. Yiddish was also seen as a corrupt form of German. Young people began to teach themselves German and there was a realisation amongst well to do Jews that Education should and could be broader. Many of them sent their sons away to new schools in Berlin and other famous cities.

From 1780, Jews had been accepted in German Universities, however, they were still restricted to just their own subjects to be studied in a purely technical sense. Once formal Jewish education was completed, it was often the case that business training followed. Jews were now seeking non-Jewish education, especially medicine. There must have been much argument between father and son as to their visions of the future! I wonder how many arguments Wolf had with his sons?

In Jewish families, girls were looked upon as not needing formal education. It was considered to be much more important to prepare them for marriage and motherhood. Females did not usually attend school, but absorbed what they could from their surroundings. With such an 'enlightened father, I imagine Wolf's daughters were pretty strong characters who would find it difficult to accept their traditional role, I can almost hear the arguments!

Even in the 'enlightened' times of Emancipation, women were excluded from studying for recognised professions such as the Law and Medicine. 'Enlightenment' did benefit women in other ways, however. They quickly began to realise there were other, new opportunities. They were the first to learn languages and began to move much more easily within 'foreign' circles. There are many records in the history books that tell of powerful Jewish women who held 'open salons' in Berlin and attracted the most noble and clever people of the day. Maybe one of Wolf's daughters was one of these women.

Although many things improved, there was still much prejudice around. There were complaints about Jews going to theatres and musical gatherings; others did not want to sit next to them. There is a story that a newspaper article appeared, citing the case of a Jew attending a public house with a Christian. The proprietor said he was welcome as far as he was concerned, but his customers objected to his Jewish company, and pressure from his customers had compelled him to refuse entry to Jews in the future. That particular Jew in question was lucky, as often no reason was given.

The more emancipated Christians found there was not so much need to disassociate themselves from Jews. There was more interest and involvement from Christians with Jews, and a higher level of interest in learning about Jewish ways of life. I have an imaginary picture of Wolf and his family keeping 'open house' for a wide variety of friends from all sorts of backgrounds, cultures and religions. I believe him to have been a very warm, accepting man whose greatest joy was to offer his friendship and hospitality to others. He definitely had some close Christian friends as he chose a man called Christian Reinhard to be the Godfather of his son, Abraham. This must have been a very unusual event.

Between 1814 and 1819 there was a new wave of anti-Jewish propaganda and animosity, but by then the Jewish community had become very strong and they were well able to weather the storm. Wolf was by now in his sixties and being a Jew, he was well used to the fact that nothing lasts forever. Some of the fire and energy of youth had maybe dissipated. Perhaps he was tired of fighting, having lived his life surrounded by prejudice and change. Possibly he was very philosophical about the whole business and as a cornerstone, used the faith of his fathers.

He would need that faith as in 1817, Abraham, at the age of twenty eight, joined the army and was to serve six years in the Archducal Light Cavalry Regiment, the Cheveaux Legers. I wonder if Wolf supported his decision to 'join up,' or if there were big family arguments? It would seem that it would have been relatively easy for him to stay at home and take some part in the family business. Although as the youngest son he would not have had much power and position in the family. Maybe that's why he decided to go!

During those years, life in the army was hard and dangerous. Soldiers lived a very rough life style. Lack of food, dirt, illness and death were all facts of everyday life. They fought hard on the battlefields and played hard in the public houses and brothels. I imagine he would certainly have been very attractive to women. Dressed in his colourful military uniform, which would most certainly have been at least two colours, with tight fitting breeches and a short cut- away jacket, trimmed with gold braid and brass buttons; knee high, kid leather boots and for a finishing touch, complimented by a tall hat complete with a plume and a swashbuckling sabre, mounted on a trusty steed. He would certainly have cut a dash in what must have been dark and dreary times. His dark, good looks can only have added to this as of course, the majority of Germans were blonde and blue-eyed. I can almost see him.

How many battles Abraham fought in, how many near escapes he had, how much he suffered, how many love affairs he experienced in that time, and how many tears he shed, will never be known by any one of us. Those are secrets that Abraham probably took with him to his grave. In any event, Abraham seems to have lived life to the full. The records show he was a really interesting character throughout his life.

Wolf must have lived constantly with the fear that he may never see his youngest son again, and also the possibility that Abraham would never live to experience and enjoy the freedom that Wolf had fought so long for. As fortune would have it, Abraham survived and finally returned to Gladenbach in 1823 (at the age of 34) and the 'Stern' family history continued.

Did Abraham return to a very different Gladenbach that he had left? That question is very difficult to answer, as life in small villages was very different to life in the towns and cities. There had been a very severe famine over all the land in 1816/17, which were known as the hunger years. Following this, all the states of what we now know as Germany, suffered a severe depression. Work and money were in short supply and disease was rife. Maybe village folk fared better than the town's folk, who knows.

Prejudice in the village could have been more or less than anywhere else. I suppose much depends on how well integrated and accepted the Stern family were. The evidence suggests that Abraham was desperate for full acceptance, as almost immediately on his return from the army he converted to Christianity. He renamed himself Christian Reinhard. This was after his Godfather and the following year in 1824, he married Anna Katharina Lang, a Christian woman from a nearby town called Romerhausen. He actually got married in her hometown. There must have been some raised eyebrows!

Whether Abraham disagreed with his father about entering the family business on his return or whether there was no place for him, I do not know. The interesting thing is that around this time he is listed as being a 'Second-hand and trinket dealer.' Perhaps he decided to set up on his own, much to the chagrin of his father I imagine, as he would have been re-affirming all the old prejudices of others by choosing this occupation and times were supposed to have changed.

From 1815 onwards, 'Industrialisation' was taking its place across the land. More people were moving from the villages to towns and cities, factories were being built and later on the railways were established. Abraham must have experienced many changes during his lifetime. Not only politically during the unification of Germany, but also culturally and economically. Many of the famous German and Austrian musicians, philosophers, artists and poets were around at this time. For instance, Goethe, (he was a famous writer and philosopher), Beethoven, Schubert and the Strauss Brothers Life must have been very exciting and interesting but at the same time extremely hard.

Abraham's marriage ended in divorce only a few years later. It is not known if they had any children. I suppose I could speculate as to the reasons for his failed marriage. Maybe they couldn't have children, maybe he couldn't settle down to village life after his exciting years in the army, maybe his wife did not like being married to a trader in second-hand goods, maybe all his efforts to deny his Jewish heritage didn't work and he still found himself on the receiving end of prejudice and locked doors, or maybe it was none of these reasons. You can almost imagine the hurt Wolf must have felt when his youngest son denied his culture and religion after he (Wolf) had fought so hard for recognition. Whatever the reasons, after his divorce, Abraham converted back to Judaism and changed his name back to Abraham Stern.

In 1828/29, the Jews of Frankfurt and Wurttemberg obtained completely free choices of occupation, Rights of Residence and Citizenship. In that same year Abraham was betrothed, for the second time to a Jewish woman called Esther Wolf. By this time Abraham was 41. Her father, like Abraham's father, was a well-known and respected Gladenbach Jewish Patron. Possibly taking the lead from what was happening in Frankfurt and Wurttemberg, Abraham applied to the Town Council for full rights of Citizenship of Gladenbach. He gave as a reason his betrothal to Esther. I wonder why he didn't extol the virtues of his own father? Maybe they did disagree about his conversion to Christianity, and were never able to heal that rift even after he converted back, or maybe marriage was a good reason.

The Town Council refused his request and he was obviously so annoyed and upset, he lodged a complaint with the District Council in Biedenkopf. This Council must have been more powerful and the Town Councils were probably answerable to them. In his complaint he outlined his curriculum vitae and his assets, which amounted to 8,000 Guilders. This was a very considerable sum relative to those times. Abraham was indeed a very rich man! The documentation he provided showed his 'Prussian' nationality. The District Council ordered the Town Council to present their report and expressed its great indignation at the unwarranted refusal. There is no further record to say whether Abraham's request was ever granted, but he apparently stayed on in Gladenbach.

Sadly, Abraham's marriage to Esther did not last long as in 1830, only two years later he married Greila Elias, the mother of his son, Simon, David's great-grandfather. I can only speculate as to what happened to Esther. As I have said, times were hard and there was much disease about. Perhaps Greila died of some awful disease. Perhaps she died in childbirth. This kind of thing happened all too often in those times.

By the year of 1830, Jews were well represented amongst the middle and upper classes. Emancipation was now fully accepted, and Wolf had lived to see his dreams of equality become reality. Later that year, having reached the grand age of eighty, (no mean feat in those days), he died, leaving all his property and wealth to his children. Abraham, by now, was probably very well established and respected. I don't know if Abraham had more children but I get a picture of him being a very hardworking, caring, family man. Even though by his old age, Abraham had married several times, he was probably involved in 'sharp business deals and political fights concerning his own, and other Jews, identity and acceptance. Following his early dabble with another religion, I believe he would, by now, have been a very committed Jew. The Sabbath would have been observed, without fail. His wife would have prepared all the wonderful dishes, in advance, that were eaten on the Sabbath and said the Sabbath prayer over the lit candles. At Passover their prayer would always have ended with the words 'next year in Jerusalem'. Devout Jews always believed they would one day go to Israel. During the hard and hungry years he may often have intoned this ancient prayer at his Synagogue: -

Hear me, Jacob, Israel, whom I have called:
I am the one, the beginning and the end.
My own hand founded the earth and spread out the skies.
Thus saith the Eternal One.
Who created the heavens and stretched them out.
Who made earth and all that grows in it,
Who gives breath to its people and spirit to those who walk in it.

In 1838, eight years after he married Greila, he was once again to experience losing a wife. On 13.4.1838, the official doctor, Doctor Deibel, confirmed the death of Abraham's wife. Perhaps he was left a widower with several children to care for and due to this, he married again. This was the fourth time! The date is not known but her name was Amalie. Amalie was born on 22nd April 1822. This would have made her around the age of eighteen if they married in 1840 and Abraham would have been fifty-one. It looks like he had chosen someone young and fit to care for him and his children, a not unusual happening for those times, or maybe he was just trying to recapture his youth. Amalie was recorded as still being alive in 1900 and by then she would have been 78. She was referred to in the records as 'Grandmother Amalie Stern', so she must have had children to Abraham. What a fit man! I hope Abraham found happiness and contentment with Amalie.

Meanwhile, further socio-economic changes were occurring which were to feed into more political upheavals. In Europe as a whole, a population expansion had been taking place since the middle of the eighteenth century - it wasn't all Abraham's efforts. Much of the population growth in Germany was rural, and the food supply of a still pre-industrial economy proved insufficient to support a growing population on the land. Food riots, rural unemployment, migration to growing towns, even immigration across the Atlantic to the land of opportunity and moving frontiers to America, were common. The growth of pauperism and the widespread existence of acute poverty running alongside the rich society, all gave rise to considerable social concern.

I can just imagine Abraham, like his father Wolf, being a champion of the poor. During the early 1840's, there were several 'mini-revolutions'. In 1846-7, a potato blight meant malnutrition and potential starvation for many, including thousands of deaths from poverty related diseases. I can see Abraham and Amalie sharing their good fortune with those less fortunate. I wonder if they literally gave food and practical help to those who needed it. At least one of the later ancestors did, as you will see.

In 1847, Bismark appeared on the political scene. Anti-Semitism began to raise its ugly head again. Bismark objected that access to everything by the Jews would be against the Christian character. For the Jewish community this must have been very difficult to deal with as for the past few years, things seemed to have been settling down, all the other political unrest having taken precedence. I imagine Abraham would have been absolutely infuriated and fought hard against such statements. However, it seems that someone, somewhere, was listened to, as in the years of 1848 1849, the all-German assembly accepted The Principle of Equality. 1848 was a year of revolution across Europe. In Germany, it was largely limited to demands for immediate improvements in wages and working conditions. I like to think that if Abraham had people working for him, he was a good and considerate employer who cared about his staff.

Although many other political changes were taking place, the most important thing was that between the years of 1866 and 1871, the Unification of the Northern Countries of Germany and then the whole Reich was brought about by the acceptance of the principle of citizenship independent of religious confession in 1869. This must have been a time for celebration for Abraham, his family, friends and all the Jews of Germany. At last it looked like they had achieved equality and they could now worship their own God publicly!

Abraham and Greila's son, Simon (he was David's great-grandfather) was born in 1833 on the 21st January. He would have grown up in those times of unrest and change. What his childhood was like, I cannot begin to imagine. Still true to form, like all the other Sterns and probably all the other Jews, he married, by our standards, quite late in life in 1874. He was forty-one years old at the time. He married Jettchen Rosenberg who was the daughter of a butcher named Isaak. She came from a place called Grossenbuseck. Jettchen was born in 1840 so would have been aged thirty-four. On the marriage certificate they were both listed as being second-hand dealers in Gladenbach.

So far, I have not been able to find a date of death for Abraham so I don't know if he was still alive when Simon married. Certainly if he was alive he would have been eighty-five. The facts seem to indicate that David's ancestors were all long livers, and modern research shows that longevity runs in families, so David should have a long life to look forward to.

Can you get the picture of the wedding? In the Synagogue under the canopy, called the Chupah, which represents the home that the couple will live in, and with so many people present - probably all the Jewish community in Gladenbach. There are references in the history books that even the Christians loved to join in on these occasions as they were so lively and entertaining - a happy release from all the day to day struggles. There would be so much dancing and singing, and everyone shouting 'Shalom' (Peace be unto you), 'Lochiem' (To life!) and 'Mazel tov' (Good Luck). It might even have resembled the wedding scene from 'Fiddler on the Roof'.

Simon and Jettchen

Simon married Jettchen in 1834. Simon died when he was seventy-four and Jettchen died when she was seventy-two. From what I can gather they had both lived long and healthy lives. Somewhere along the line, I think it is possible that Simon changed his occupation from being a second-hand dealer - not respected at all - to being a butcher, which was a well respected occupation. The reason I think this is because his son Adolph, eventually became a well-known butcher in the village. Maybe Simon inherited a business from his wife's father and then passed it on to Adolph. They are both buried in the same grave in the Jewish cemetery in Gladenbach. When Simon and Jettchen died, the ages of their children would have been Lina at 35 years old, who was the village midwife, and later a doctor, all in a time when it was difficult for women to attend University; Adolph at 34, and Sally at 32.

The custom of placing stones on a grave probably draws upon pagan customs, but the stones also symbolize the permanence of the memory of the Jewish person who has died. The practice of burying the dead with flowers is almost as old as humanity. Even in prehistoric caves some burial sites have been found with evidence that flowers were used in interment. But Jewish authorities have often objected to bringing flowers to the grave. There are scattered Talmudic mentions of spices and twigs used in burial (Berakhot 43a, Betzah 6a www. My Jewish learning 2015), yet the prevailing view was that bringing flowers smacks of a pagan custom, so stones were seen as the here and now and seen as a permanent reminder of the Jew. When we went to the Jewish graveyard in Gladenbach there was evidence that this custom is still carried on and yet there were no stones on Simon and Jettchen's grave.

Throughout all these years, some 150 to be exact, this particular Family Stern had always lived in Gladenbach. However, somehow, some of the wealth and property, (remember the house and stabling that belonged to Wolf), must have either been lost or passed on to the eldest son. Again, you need to remember that Abraham was the youngest son. By this time, the family lived at 10 Burgstrasse, a large house on one of the main streets in the village. This was classed as the better part to live in, and was not amongst the rest of the Jewish community.

They later lived on a street that rose up a hill towards the Jewish cemetery, and halfway up the street there was a small synagogue, destroyed during World War 2. I don't know the correct name of this street, but I do know it was, and still is commonly referred to as 'Judengasse', the street of the Jews. We have been there! Sadly, the house on Burgstrasse no longer exists, but there is a photograph of it, and the family continued to live there for a number of years until Adolph and Sarah left. The shop was at the back, so later on it was no hardship for customers to go round the back!

House on Burgerstrasse

Adolph and Sarah

Although there is no definite date for Adolph's meeting with Sarah or their marriage, records show he must have married before or during 1900. The marriage was not recorded in Gladenbach so he must have got married somewhere else. His wife was called Sarah Stern even before she married him. I can only guess that 'Stern', by this time, was a fairly common name. I do know that before the Second World War there were five families named Stern in Gladenbach. This meant that upon marrying Adolph, Sarah didn't actually change her name. Sarah was from a place called Neustadt which was not that far away, and she was born in 1873, the same year as Simon. Taking the average age of previous marriages into account, I suppose twenty-seven was looked upon as an early marriage.

There are no records to date to show if Lina or Sally (Adolph's sisters) ever married. There is a record, however, which shows that Lina was still living with her parents in 1911. She would by then have been thirty-nine years old, so I can only conclude that she became a doctor and never married. Adolph is listed as being a butcher and tradesman, which was a well respected trade for a Jew. If you look at his children's Birth Certificates, you can see he is called Von Metzger Adolph Stern. 'Von Metzger' means butcher.

Anti-Semitism still existed in the village and both Adolph and Sarah must have had to deal with it on a regular basis. The build up to the 1914 - 1918 War can't have helped as once again, Jews were used as 'scapegoats'. Adolph always wanted to be known as a German first. A German, who was fiercely patriotic and happened to be of Jewish descent. He fought in what has now become known as The Great War, which was World War 1.

I don't know where or for how long, but it must have been pretty awful, just as it was for British soldiers. My own grandfather was away fighting in France for four years.

Possibly Adolph was away for that long too. Whichever side they were on they were both just essentially obeying orders and fighting for their country and what they believed in. The horrors of war are difficult to understand. Who knows what Adolph witnessed and had to suffer? At least he survived the war. During his time fighting, Adolph made a very close Christian friend, also called Adolph, during his time fighting who was later to try and persuade him to leave Gladenbach to no avail.

Adolph and Sarah had five children. Selma who was born in 1902, then Karl born in 1904, Klara born in 1905, and Siegfried born in 1907. Siegfried died at the age of two, at the time when there was a severe outbreak of diphtheria, so he may well have died of this. Then Dora was born in 1911. When Adolph was called away to fight, he must have left Sarah with four children all under the age of twelve, the youngest being only three. I imagine she must have had a difficult time managing and surviving. Army pay would have been pathetic just as it was for English soldiers. Put this together with trying to keep a business going, caring for all the children, never knowing if she would see Adolph again and probably having to deal with the attitudes and prejudice of others, it must have been a nightmare. I feel that Sarah must have been a very strong woman who held family values close to her heart. All the children had a very happy and carefree childhood, but in 1933, as young adults, things were to change for them all.

Jewish traditions were very important to them all as a family; festival and dietary laws were observed, and the family regularly attended 'schul' at the local synagogue. Saturday, the Sabbath, was important too, and was celebrated each week by the whole family. They were considered to be quite financially comfortable. The girls were trained in all household duties and also as seamstresses. Karl was trained as a tailor. Apparently, Selma was 'the clever one,' and they did not know what to do with her. Selma and Klara were inseparable as sisters and did everything together, including looking for boyfriends and going out as a foursome.

From what I can gather, life in Gladenbach was, around this time, fairly happy and supportive. It seems that everyone knew everyone else and it was quite a close-knit community. Adolph and Sarah were looked upon as middle-class, but at the same time caring and giving, as well as important members of the community. Adolph made a point of making special sausages, amongst other things, to give to poor people who could not afford to buy meat. They were both well known as very kind, accepting people who were always ready to share what they had. As a couple they were well respected and had a wide circle of friends, not all of them Jewish. It was later confirmed how well respected and loved Adolph and Sarah were, and how kind they were to others who were less fortunate than themselves.

Then, in 1933, the sands of time were running out for the Stern family, as it was also for thousands, nay millions of Jews all over the world. In January of that year, Adolph Hitler was appointed Chancellor of Germany. Until then, gossip and speculation had been rife, but with no real happenings, so this had engendered a false sense of security. The watchword was 'hold your tongue' and pitting neighbour against neighbour was encouraged. In February 1933, the S.A. and S.S. were born. (S.A. being the Sturmabteilung - Assault Division/Storm Troopers, or Brownshirts. S.S. being the Sturmstaffel - Storm Squadron, then later called Schutzstaffel - Protection Squad). In April, Nazis boycotted Jewish shops and businesses. For the Stern family, this would have meant each member trying to believe that this was not happening. Also, on reading the newspapers, they would have realised that prejudice against the Jews was rife, and that the State was encouraging it. They had to learn to live with loudspeakers on the streets and State controlled radio. It must have felt like living on a time bomb. Regardless of this, Adolph Stern was heard to say "Es wird nicht alles so heiss gegessen, wie es gekkocht wird," "the bark is worse than the bite." He is also reputed to have said, "We passed through the Red Sea and we shall pass through the brown shit!" He prophesied that because they had a strong sense of Jewish identity, strength of tradition would continue in the face of rapid social change, and that everything would soon be OK. He was heard to say, "We do not know any Fatherland but Germany and our Mother tongue!" This proved to be a love that was to become fateful. Himmler was credited with saying, "Jews are unbearable to my soul and my psyche. Rid Europe of all Jews." It was he, and then others, who originally pushed for all Jews to emigrate. The State then set up offices for Jews to get travel documents, at a price, to enable them to travel and leave Germany.

The first major step, eventually leading to the 'Final Solution', was the attempt on the part of the Nazi regime to force the Jews to emigrate out of Germany. Hitler's motivation seems to have been two-fold: to ensure the racial purity of Germany and to create lebensraum, 'living space,' for German nationals of Aryan blood. Throughout the 1930's Nazi domestic policy was aimed at stripping Jews of any citizenship rights, and any economic and political rights. This first step towards a 'final solution of the Jewish problem', as far as the Nazi's believed, was the complete dehumanization of Jews. Even then, Adolph Stern believed the Nazi regime would not last, and he was reluctant to leave, to go anywhere, saying that he and Sarah were too old for a new life, that their roots were deep in Gladenbach, and that they had many belongings which they had preserved from the 1920s and 1930s.

The girls by this time were 31, 28 and 22. Karl was 29 and big brother to the three sisters, even though he was younger than Selma by two years. He also agreed with anything his father said. During 1933 Adolph Stern's customers, Jews and Christians alike were told "Do not shop at the Plague Stall," and so they came to the back door of his shop to ensure no one would see them. The first workers to really suffer and be out of work were civil servants. They, the Jewish Civil Servants, were classed as vermin and unable to do the job properly. A lot of other non-Jews suffered too. So once again, the Jews were under threat.

By 1933, Hitler had managed to convince many people of his ideas. The Jewish people were amongst the first to suffer, and from all the material I have read, it seems that it was not that difficult for Hitler to convince people. All the old prejudices were still there under the surface, and it didn't help that, generally speaking, the Jews who were successful in business, were better off than many others, and as such had quite a lot of power, especially in the economy of Germany. The German people were trapped in a deep financial depression. Many people were starving; it was almost impossible to even buy a loaf of bread. Unemployment was high, and social problems were rife. At the time Hitler came along, people were looking for a saviour, and early that year Hitler 'proved' himself to the people by putting people to work, building roads and railways and generally improving the lot of many individuals.

From 1935 onwards, offensive slogans began to appear in Christian shop windows, the Jewish cafes and houses were smeared with shit and paint. Signs that said 'Jews not wanted here' announced the German people's feelings. There were effigies of Jews burned in the street. Kosher butchers were attacked non-stop and there were many who believed that the right place for a Jewish butcher was a concentration camp. At livestock markets the SS often attacked and cattle were set free to run amok.

Having suffered some of this, life in the village became more and more difficult, and from 1935 Adolph and Sarah encouraged the three sisters, Selma, Klara and Dora; Karl saw it as his duty to stay, to leave the village and move to Frankfurt until everything calmed down and returned to normal. This was in the belief that it would be easier for them to keep a low profile in a large city where they were not known. Dora went in 1936 but Selma and Klara did not go to the big city until May of 1938. In fact, it was Klara's birthday on the day she went. Many thousands of Jews did exactly the same thing. Adolph firmly believed that he was witnessing yet another bout of anti-Semitism that would soon die down, after all, he and his ancestors before him were no strangers to it.

His favourite saying was – 'Question – 'Why does a Jew always wear his hat?' Answer – 'Because he always wants to be ready to move on.' The familiar held no fears for him. How could he have even suspected things would turn out as they did?

I don't especially want to recount all the happenings there were in the years leading up to and during the war in 1939 - 1945, but 1938 seems to have been the worst year ever. So many laws were made and so many people were sent to concentration camps. In the summer month of August, all Jews were required to have their Passports stamped with a large red 'J,' and all Jews were required to change their name to Sarah for women, and Israel for men. There is proof of this only for Dora and Karl, but all the other family members must have been subjected to this. These must have been terrible times to live in.

Somewhere around this time, Adolph's best friend (Adolph, a close friend who had fought in the first world war with him), wrote to him, begging Adolph and his family to leave Germany. Friend Adolph had emigrated to America two years earlier, and was doing well. From the outside looking in, he could obviously see the writing on the wall. He even offered to pay all their travels costs. By this time, Jews were only allowed to take a very small amount of money out of the country, having to leave behind their houses and property. "Just walk out and come!" friend Adolph said. He also offered to provide them with a house in America. But Adolph Stern was very stubborn, refusing to believe that he and his wife were in danger. He also refused point blank to leave his birthplace and his home, saying that he was too old for change, that he was born and bred in Gladenbach, and that nobody was going to make him leave! This was in the summer of 1938.

In January 1939, Hitler threatened the Jews directly in the Reichstag speech, which was broadcast everywhere and in the February, all Jews had to hand over all the gold and silver items that they had. In September of that year, the Nazi's invaded Poland and all Jews were forbidden to be outdoors after 8pm in winter and 9pm in Summer. It was in September 1939 that Great Britain declared war on Germany. The newspaper, Der Sturmer, (Wikipedia: Der Sturmer 2015) published that, "The Jewish people ought to be exterminated root and branch. Then the plague of pests would have disappeared in Poland at one stroke."

Adolph and Sarah stayed on in Gladenbach right up until June 1940, and by then they could take no more. Official records show that they left the village together on 17.06.1940 being the last Jews to leave. By then, Germany had been at war for ten months, invading Poland, Denmark, France, Belgium, Luxembourg and Holland. Later they were to invade Czechoslovakia. During this time, many Jews, along with many others, had been incarcerated in concentration camps and died there.

They originally went to live with Selma in Frankfurt, thinking it would be easier to get lost in a big city. In September of 1941 it was decreed that Yellow Stars were to be worn by all Jews. Because Adolph had fought in the Great War for Germany, he thought that he and his immediate family would be protected. How wrong he was. They 'existed' for quite a long time in Frankfurt but sadly, they were arrested in Frankfurt in late 1942, and then taken to Theriesenstadt concentration camp on a cattle train. Terezin was its name until the German's changed it. A key part of the Nazi plans for the New Order of Europe was the extermination of all Jews within the reach of Hitler's Germany. Theriesenstadt was created and opened on 24th November, 1941. This was the camp or small fortress that was said to be Hitler's gift to the Jews but was to become an important cog in the 'Final Solution of the Jewish Question', the euphemistic Nazi title for the Jewish genocide.

The date they arrived at the concentration camp 'Ghetto Theresienstadt' was the 16th September 1942. This particular camp was known as a transitional camp and was rumoured to be especially for older Jews who were German, and to whom the state owed something. From there, prisoners were either moved on to the death camps of Auschwitz and Buchenwald, they died there in Theresienstadt. The mass murder and cremation of Jews was a daily part of life in Theresienstadt. Desperate hygiene and health conditions and the availability of decent food in the small fortress deteriorated day by day.

Street plan of Thereisenstadt

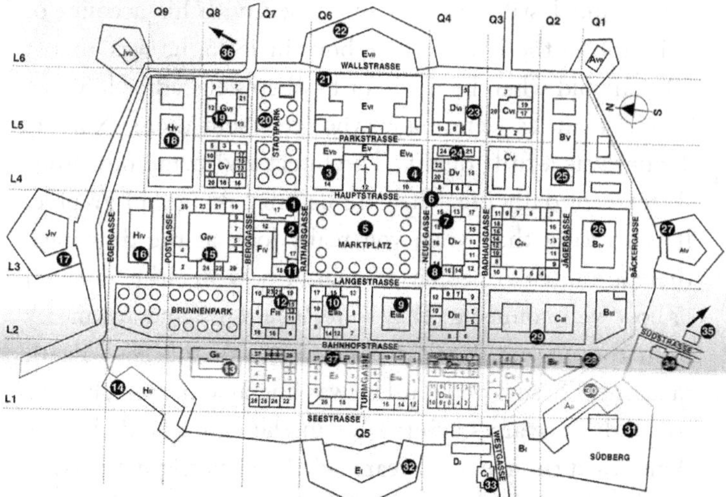

1 *L 417* Today's Ghetto Museum. This former Terezín school served as a home for boys.

2 *Q 619* The Terezín Town Hall was the seat of what was called Bank of the Jewish Self-Administration and other offices; it was also the venue of various cultural performances.

3 *L 414* The building of the former Fortress Headquarters first served as the SS Camp Headquarters, later as a post-office and a youth home.

4 *L 410* A dormitory for young girls where drawing lessons were given by Friedl Dicker-Brandejsová.

5 *Marktplatz* Fenced off and inaccessible to the inmates, the main square was turned into a park opened to the prisoners during Terezín's "beautification campaign".

6 *L 415* One of the stores that were located primarily in the L 4 and L 3 Streets.

7 *Q 418* A cafe was opened in this house in December 1942.

8 *Q 414, 416* The buildings housing the SS Camp Headquarters. The infamous bunkers were in the cellars.

9 *L 311* The Engineering Barracks, home for elderly inmates and a makeshift hospital.

10 *L 315* The seat of the Ghetto guards who helped maintain order in Terezín.

11 *L 318* Home for small kids and children of early school-age. Terezín kindergarten. It also housed a kitchen for children.

12 *Block F III* Homes for children and apprentices.

13 *Block G II* The seat of a Czech gendermerie unit guarding the camp.

14 *Block H II* Known as Bauhof, this was the site of craftsmen's workshops.

15 *L 324* Called Viktoria-Haus, this building served as a canteen and flats for the staff of the SS Camp Headquarters.

16 *Block H IV* The Bodenbach Barracks – prisoners' dormitory, in the middle of 1943 given over to the needs of the staff of the RSHA Archives from Berlin.

17 *Block J IV* The Aussig Barracks – a central warehouse of clothing and luggage seized from the inmates.

18 *Block H V* The Dresden Barracks – a dormitory for women prisoners, with the camp's prison in its cellar.

19 *Block G VI* Homes for suckling infants and small children. A library with a reading room, and a theater hall were set up in one of the houses.

20 *Stadtpark* A children's pavilion was built during the "beautification campaign" and the park was turned into a playground.

21 *Block E VI* The Hohenelbe Barracks – central hospital and baths.

22 *Block E VII* The Kavalír Barracks served the accommodation of the elderly and mentally ill inmates.

23 *Block D VI* The town's former brewery was turned into a disinfecting station.

24 Former army riding hall housed a mechanical joiner's workshop.

25 *Block B V* The Magdeburg Barracks – seat of the Council of Elders and the central office for the Jewish Self-Administration. Today this building houses Terezín's Meeting Center and attic theater. Visitors can view a replica of the dormitory from the time of the Ghetto as well as permanent exhibitions devoted to different walks of cultural life in the Ghetto.

26 *Block B IV* The Hannover Barracks – a dormitory for men fit for work.

27 *Block A IV* Terezín's bakery and main food warehouse.

28 *Bahnhofstrasse* Part of the railway siding leading from the Bohušovice Railway Station to Terezín, built by the inmates in 1942-1943. This provided for faster handling of transports to and from Terezín.

29 *Block C III* The Hamburg Barracks - a dormitory for women. In 1943 mostly Dutch prisoners were accommodated in this building, which also housed the main center for handling incoming and outgoing transports, the so-called šlojska (sluice or checkpoint).

30 *Block A II* The Jäger Barracks – a dormitory for elderly inmates and a quarantine.

31 *Südberg* The Southern Hill – prisoners were allowed to enter this part of town in 1943 when a sports ground was built there.

32 *Block E I* The Sudeten Barracks – the Ghetto's first building and a dormitory for men. It was vacated in the summer of 1943, the building then housed part of the RSHA Archives transferred from Berlin.

33 *Objekt C I* Sokol gym – initially used as a hospital ward, it was turned into what was billed as the Ghetto's "Community Center" during the "beautification campaign".

34 *Südstrasse* The Mortuary and Ceremonial Halls. The Columbarium is located opposite.

35 The Jewish Cemetery with Crematorium.

36 The Memorial site by the Ohře river where the ashes of the cremated prisoners were thrown into the river at the Nazi orders in 1944.

37 Prayer room from the time of the Ghetto.

Ghetto Museum, Magdeburg Barracks & Prayer room from the time of the Ghetto

Visiting hours	daily, throughout the year
winter season	Nov 1 – March 31: 9 a.m. – 5:30 p.m.
summer season	April 1 – Oct 31: 9 a.m. – 6 p.m.
closed on	Dec 24 – 26, Jan 1

Columbarium, Ceremonial Halls and Central Mortuary

Visiting hours	
daily, throughout the year	9 a.m. – 5 p.m.
closed on	Dec 24 – 26, Jan 1

Crematorium

Visiting hours all year round except Saturdays	
winter season	Nov 1 – March 31: 10 a.m. – 4 p.m.
summer season	April 1 – Oct 31: 10 a.m. – 5 p.m.
closed on	Dec 24 – 26, Jan 1

Address: Ghetto Museum Terezín, Komenského ulice, CZ-411 55 Terezín • Telephone: +420-416 782 576-7 • Fax: +420-416 782 300 • E-mail: manager@pamatnik-terezin.cz • http://www.pamatnik-terezin.cz

Established in October 1991, the Ghetto Museum now houses a permanent exhibition tracing the history of the Ghetto and portraying the individual aspects of everyday life of the inmates. Sightseeing tours include displays of works of art made by both adult and young prisoners. • Documentaries are screened in the cinema hall. • Specialized literature, promotional items and videocassettes on Terezín may also be purchased here. • A permanent exhibition is also housed in the Crematorium.

I have a photocopy of part of Norbert Troller's book, 'Theresienstadt - Hitler's Gift to the Jews', but it's been so long and I can't remember where I got it from! I remember being, and I still am, very impressed with his account of daily life in the camp. Being born in 1896, he was almost 50 years old when he was sent to Theresienstadt. He was a 'clever' man, as were many who were sent there. Norbert Troller was a fully qualified architect and made numerous sketches of daily life. They are heartbreaking and graphic. It is striking that when you really look at the drawings, there are faces of people, no matter how wealthy, talented or how well-connected they were, would not find any mercy from the pitiless, faceless malevolence of the Nazi death machine. He survived until he was liberated in 1945, having spent three years staying alive in the camp, and died in America at the age of 90 years old. Troller's relatives died in camps all over Europe much like the members of the Stern family, each one not knowing what had happened to the other. Only one of his sons survived, as far as I can find out, only to commit suicide in the late 60's in California. I am including excerpts from his memoirs as I think he deserves recognition. I have only included some of his words, mixed with my own; that is to say, it is not full of his direct quotes.

Pure evil is difficult to imagine. The exact source of the terrifying logic by which the Nazi's waged their war of extermination of the Jews of Europe is unthinkable. In that period between 1939 and 1945, over one thousand years of 'Jewishness' and all that it stood for were ground almost into oblivion. The list of names will remain in our memories forever: Treblinka, Belsen, Auschwitz, Sobibor and the other death camps. Most of the Jews who were murdered in concentration camps went to their deaths without resistance, they were holding on to some slim hope that 'they were different' and their captors would treat them well.

Between November 1941 and April 1945, 140,000 people entered Theresiensadt and when the Russian army liberated the camp in 1945 there were just over one third who had survived. The Nazi's plan, that while they were isolating the Jews from the rest of the populations of Europe, whilst they were murdering them in every conceivable way – by shooting, gassing, starvation, disease – the leadership really thought they could keep the final solution a secret from the rest of the world!

Theresienstadt was created particularly for the elderly German speaking Jews who had fought on the side of Germany in WW1, pensioners and older people. Although on the face of it, the city was organised, had cultural events and a Council of Elders, the Nazi's knew that the people would not survive starvation, disease, poor sanitary conditions and the rest, especially the older people, and therefore would die in their hundreds, thus fulfilling with the extermination concept.

Troller writes, "Human nature has a tendency to be optimistic; we try to interpret the misfortunes of others in such a way that we believe that misfortune will pass us by because we are 'special cases'." (Troller 1991) In contrast, he writes of the "stark terror" of the Nazi round-up of their victims. The loud voices of the S.S. barking commands, "Raus, raus, line up." "We get up, line up, with rucksack, toolkit, carryall, canteen filled with water, screaming children pull their mother's this way and that. We move downstairs, line up in rows of four and move out of the gate. It is completely dark." (Troller 1991) "Goodbye was said to friends whom we had learned to love, and when they left we tried to delude ourselves with the thought these are

German Jews from the Reich, probably they will be resettled as German Jews somewhere in the east."

"It is difficult to remember the frightful pressures to which one succumbed at a time when survival seemed impossible. It was a time when we were forced to make sudden decisions daily. There was no time to consider one's own feelings; there was only the constant pressure to act with lightening speed; no time to consider eventual pros and cons."

On arrival at Theresienstadt, with their equipment and luggage nearly intact, Adolph and Sarah were to see their belongings confiscated there and then, and they saw them disappear. It must have been a tragic experience. The group of people who suffered most, in my opinion, were the elderly and infirm. This group had a hard time trying to avoid starvation. They could not work so were therefore on minimum rations. The really old ones were in a desperate situation, they starved. They used to stand by the queue of more able people, and politely request of them if they were going to eat their soup? The soup was made from nothing and was inedible. Troller says, "They were eager customers for the so called lentil soup; it was a pitiful sight." Their weight loss was rapid and the old [1]people would contract diarrhoea, and unstoppable enteritis. They had to go to the hospital – miserable and stinking – where they quite literally 'shit out' their lives.

The first thing Adolph and Sarah saw when they arrived at Theriesenstadt, written over the gates in large black letters, was 'ARBIGHT MACHT FREI- WORK LIBERATES.'

A photo of the gate 'Arbiet Macht Frei'

Adolph and Sarah must have seen this, and I can't believe that they would have believed it. There were a number of old and powerless prisoners in the Theriesenstadt Ghetto, whose fate was especially hard, and Adolph and Sarah were part of this. They were assigned to the attics as they were both 69. The attics were just that, up many stairs and all the elderly Jews had to sleep together in dormitories.

A picture of old people in attics

A drawing by Bedřich Fritta: The "homes" of the elderly prisoners in the attic

Sarah, after her arrival at Theresienstadt, lived only six weeks, her date of death was recorded as 2nd November 1942. Adolph survived longer and continued on until 4th December 1943. Sarah was 69 and Adolph was 70 when they died. What horrors they were subjected to; what atrocities they witnessed, and exactly how they died no-one will ever know. Those details were not included on their Death Certificates. They were both listed as 'cardiac failure'.

The years of Nazi occupation of the Czech lands were the most tragic chapter of the 'small fortress'. Theresienstadt had been a police prison of Prague's Gestapo, and was established as early as June 1940. Roughly thirty-two thousand prisoners went through its overcrowded cells.

Over the years in Theresienstadt, famine, epidemics, inhuman treatment and executions ended more than two and a half thousand lives.

A poem by Jaroslav Seifert was selected for the beginning of a booklet, bought at Theresienstadt. I thought I would include it for everyone to read.

TO THE DEAD

A grave amongst graves, who can tell it apart,
Time has long swept away the dead faces.
Testimonies, so evil and terrible to the heart,
We took with us to these dark rotting places.

Only the night and the howl of the wind
Will sit on the graves' corners,
Only a patch of grass, a bitter weed
Before May bears some flowers ....

Jaroslav Seifert
From - Terezin – Places of suffering and braveness.
Booklet bought at Terezin in 2004

Influences between 1933 and 1939.

During the 1930's, especially from 1930, Hitler and his views were very influential. The Nazis boycotted Jewish shops and businesses, and the Nazi's issued a decree that anyone who was not of Aryan descent had to admit or declare it. This was especially pertinent to Jewish people, and included parent or grandparent generation in classifying the descendent as non-Aryan.

The Gestapo was born and the Nazis passed a law that anyone who was found to have a 'genetic defect' must be forcibly sterilised. Among other terrible things, they burned a particular book. Before I tell you what happened to each of the family members, I will try and set the scene of what it was like to live in Germany at that time as a Jew. I have given you a flavour of 1933, but sadly it got much worse.

There was a popular daily newspaper called Der Sturmer (The Attacker). This newspaper was owned by a man called Streicher who wanted the paper to appeal to the common man, to the worker with little time to read. Der Sturmer's articles used short sentences and a simple vocabulary. Ideas were repeated and headlines grabbed a reader's attention. The cartoons used were easily understood, and a famous cartoonist was behind the drawing of anti-Semitic caricatures, where he portrayed Jews with large hooked noses, bulging eyes, unshaven, short and fat. He often drew them depicted as vermin or snakes, and the paper was filled with stories about scandal, sex and crime. Though perhaps based on truth, the articles were often exaggerated and the facts were distorted. The articles were written by only a couple of people, Streicher being one of them. The paper continued to be printed throughout the war years with its final edition appearing on February, 1945. The ordinary German believed what was written and thus Der Sturmer was very influential in people's attitudes towards Jews.

All the things that happened between 1933 – 1938 made Selma and Klara think they must leave their small village of Gladenbach. In 1933, the Nazis had burned the Reichstag building, creating an atmosphere of crisis. They opened Dachau concentration camp and swiftly followed this with Buchenwald, Sachsenhausen and Ravensbruck which was for women only.

1934

So much happened during this year that it is too much to tell you. However, among the edicts:

Jews were banned from the German labour front, were not allowed Health Insurance, were banned from getting legal qualifications and the German people gave Hitler a 90% YES vote, approving his new powers.

1935

Many things happened in 1935 also. But the most important were that Jews were banned from serving in the military, Nazi's forced women to have an abortion if she was likely to pass on a hereditary disease and the Nuremberg Race Laws against the Jews were passed.

1936

1936 saw the Gestapo being placed above the law, the Olympic Games being held in Berlin, and an office was established for combating homosexuality and abortions.

1937

Jews were banned from many professional occupations including teaching, medicine, dentistry and accountancy. They were also denied tax reductions and child allowance.

1938

This was the year Nazi troops invaded Austria. At the time, there were 200,000 Jews living there. The S.S. were placed in charge of Jewish affairs in Vienna. Mauthausen concentration camp was established, and the Nazi's prohibited any Jew to own any business.

If you have a further interest in what happened in Germany during those years, you can read that for yourself. I find it too awful to talk about in detail, and I am sure you are aware of many of the events. They must have been terrible times to live in.

From here on, I will tell you the stories of each individual, and what happened to them as far as I can tell.

Selma – the clever one.

Selma carried on alone in Frankfurt, working for a doctor until she was arrested. Because the doctor was a non-Jew, she managed to escape the notice of the Gestapo for a long time. She was politically active, and was proud of her Jewishness, but hid it. In September 1942, she was arrested and sent to a little known political prisoners' concentration camp, which masqueraded under the name of a labour camp run by the S.S. in Riga, in the East of Prussia. She was many kilometres from home or anyone she knew. She survived for almost two years there.

Then, on 23rd August 1944, she was sent to Stutthof Camp.

A map of where the concentration camps were

Sztutowo is the name of a fisherman's village, located thirty four kilometres northeast of Gdansk and Danzig, and three kilometres from the Baltic coast. With the German invasion of Poland, Sztutowo became known as Stutthof, and entered the halls of history as the infamous concentration camp. The site chosen was conveniently situated, with good connections to Danzig. The triangle of the Baltic Sea, the Vistula and Nogat Rivers, all served the practical purpose of preventing prisoners from escaping.

Before the war, a wooden home for the elderly was situated in a forest near to the village of Stutthof. This site was seen as ideal, because of its impression of quiet peacefulness and beauty. However, the ground was very wet, and under the thin layer of sand were marshes and peat bogs, which made it difficult to build on. Also, the water in this area lacked lime, which is necessary for the control of harmful bacteria, and the resulting high level of bacteria in the water proved deadly for some prisoners.

In the middle of August 1939, a detachment of prisoners was brought to this area, who were from the Schiesstange Prison in Danzig. They fenced in a small clearing, and erected temporary wooden constructions. One group from this detachment was responsible for organising the camp. According to the camp's accounts, which were scrupulously maintained, by the end of March 1940, almost 3,000 Reichs marks had been invested in Stutthof. The camp had also been expanded to accommodate several thousand prisoners. It was heard to be said that, 'To the sounds of striking axes and crashing trees, a huge encampment is taking shape in the forest near the coast. Columns of emaciated men (forced labour?) sag under the weight of bricks and iron bars, huge pine trunks cut into their shoulders, crushing them down to the ground'. Stutthof was the first Nazi concentration camp to be established on Polish soil, and the last to be dissolved. It grew from four to a hundred and twenty hectares, and from 250 prisoners to a maximum of 52,000 prisoners at one time, the SS staff and guards numbering 1,056 by 1 January 1945.

Stutthof was not immediately granted the status of a State concentration camp. For three years it came under the Danzig and Gdansk police and initially was a camp for 'civil prisoners,' then later a labour camp, being called the Sonderlager Stutthof. From January 1942 the camp, which initially held three to four thousand prisoners, expanded rapidly. Prior to the expansion, the camp – later called the 'Old Camp' – had consisted of eight barracks for prisoners, a workshop, stores, baths and hospital. The number of nationalities of the prisoners increased, and the social structure of the camp changed with the influx of new transports. The first group of 450 Jews from the Free City of Danzig arrived on 17th September 1939.

Selma survived in Stutthof Camp for about four months. There, amongst other things, she would have suffered the indignity of being stripped naked of all her clothing, had her head shaved, and a number tattooed on her arm. Her prisoner number was 70550.

It was an accepted custom that when each group of new arrivals entered the camp through the main gate, the so-called 'Death Gate', the first formality completed by the political department was a brutal welcoming by the SS officer. "From now on you are no longer a person, you are a number. All your rights have been left outside the gate – you are left with only one, and that you are free to do – leave through that chimney." Newly arriving prisoners were grouped in the 'Old Camp' square; here, they sometimes waited a whole day or even longer, irrespective of the weather or time of year.

Prisoners were beaten before they were entered on the camp register. They were forced to strip on the camp square and give all their possessions to the SS officers. This was followed by the shaving of heads of both men and women, then the body-search for hidden valuables, and then finally a bath. The prisoners were then issued with camp clothing and a number, and their personal details recorded. This happened to all who arrived as prisoners.

This was followed by a period of quarantine in Blocks 17, 18, and 19 of the 'New Camp,' which lasted two to four weeks. The prisoners did not work whilst in quarantine. In the morning they performed drill under the supervision of the block or barracks chief, whilst in the afternoon there were various records to be completed, particularly for the 'arbeitseinsatz', i.e. the allocation of forced labour. After quarantine, the prisoner was assigned to a barrack in the 'New Camp,' where he or she was to sleep, and also assigned to a particular work commando. Each barrack was divided into two equal parts, A and B. Each part had a vestibule, washroom, lavatory, dayroom and sleeping quarters. The latter was furnished with three-storey bunks, which had paper mattresses filled with wood shavings, similar pillows and cotton blankets.

Hunger also played a leading part in the extermination of prisoners. For dinner, the prisoners would hurriedly swallow a bowl of soup made from turnip, carrot or cabbage scraps. For breakfast and supper, they received a piece of bread with a tiny portion of margarine or jam, supplemented with a mug of ersatz black coffee.

Disease also played a part in many deaths. A killer was Typhus, which was common in the camp. There were several epidemics in 1942, Spring of 1943, then the most serious one at the end of Summer and the Autumn of 1944. Even if the medical staff of the camp wanted to help the prisoners to regain their health, they were, to all intent and purposes, helpless in the face of this and other diseases. Those who fell sick did not die just from the illness; the incurables or chronically ill, such as those with tuberculosis, were murdered by means of injections of phenol, or drowning in the bath at night.

The camp doctor had the right of selection to the gas chamber. The SS had to think up new tricks to deceive the Jews, and in thinking they were fooling the victims, they wore railway uniforms, and carried flags and whistles, the purpose being to transport prisoners to Auschwitz, or gas them in the special train wagons.

In the camp of Stutthof, those prisoners who managed to endure the starvation, excessive work, beatings, and disease might still be killed either by a shot in the back of the head, or be gassed in the gas chamber. Many prisoners were executed by public hanging, which was meant to serve as a warning to others. This was carried out on a scaffold, initially erected near the crematorium, and then later erected in the parade ground in the New Camp. Executions usually took place just before dinner, on a scaffold set up between barracks 12 and 13. The scaffold consisted of two vertical beams, connected by a cross-beam on which two rings were hung, through which nooses were pulled. The condemned prisoners had to climb up a small ladder onto a plank set one metre above the ground. This plank was then snatched from under the victims by means of a rope.

One survivor of new arrivals is quoted as saying, "We arrived in a horrifying physical state, usually from other camps, mainly Auschwitz, to die here. We plodded on and on fatigued, with black faces, hair growing from their skin in bristle. We wore neither jumpers nor jackets, only torn summer dresses, through the tears in which our grey bodies could be seen. We were without vests, gaunt with their pointed shoulders, sunken chests – we were more like some weird ugly birds. In some of the prisoners' hands they gripped pieces of bread, but were unable to eat. Were they aware where they were once more being taken?" (www.stutthofcamp)

A total of about 50,000 Jews from various European countries passed through Stutthof during 1945. Whilst Stutthof Camp was not called a death camp like Sobibor or Treblinka, in theory, it served its purpose for the Nazis during World War 2, and was mainly a prison for political agitators. What has now become available is a massive, filmed collection of Stutthof records, totalling three hundred and five reels of film.

Whatever happened to Selma between arriving on the 23rd August 1944, and her death on 21st December of that year, I can't say. But whatever happened, she obviously suffered much, and died (having never married), without knowing what had happened to members of her family. The reason for her death is recorded as 'cardiac weakness'. I suspect she ended her life in the gas chambers, as 'cardiac arrest' was often the reason given for this kind of death. She may have been shot or hung, or she may have died of Typhus or Cholera, which was rife in all camps. Treatment was so harsh that an estimated 75,000 to 80,000 prisoners died there from hunger, or disease, or transportation to Auschwitz, to inevitable death.

It came to light after the war that one of the worst crimes committed by the Nazis was there in Stutthof. Professor Rudolf Spanner, an SS officer and 'scientist', was the owner of a small soap factory located in Danzig. In

1940, he invented a process to produce soap from human fat. This 'product' was called R.J.S. - "Reines Judische Fett" - which means Pure Jewish Fat. Hundreds of inmates were executed for the production of this soap. Rudolf Spanner was very proud of his invention. According to the testimonies of some survivors, Spanner used to spend hours and hours admiring his invention. At the liberation, the Allies discovered chambers full of the corpses of people who had been used for the production of the soap.

Reflections on Stuttof Camp

◄|CONTENTS|| PRINT

STUTTHOF

In September 1939, the Germans established the Stutthof camp in a wooded area west of Stutthof (Sztutowo), a town about 22 miles east of Danzig (Gdansk). The area was secluded: to the north was the Bay of Danzig, to the east the Vistula Bay, and to the west the Vistula River. The land was very wet, almost at sea level. The camp was situated along the Danzig-Elbing highway on the way to the popular Baltic Sea resort town of Krynica Morska.

Originally, Stutthof was a civilian internment camp under the Danzig police chief. In November 1941, it became a "labor education" camp, administered by the German Security Police. Finally, in January 1942, Stutthof became a regular concentration camp.

The original camp (known as the old camp) was surrounded by barbed-wire fences. In 1943, the camp was enlarged and a new camp was constructed alongside the earlier one. It was surrounded by electrified barbed-wire fences. The camp staff consisted of SS guards and, after 1943, Ukrainian auxiliaries.

Major Nazi camps in Europe, January 1944
See maps

Tens of thousands of people, perhaps as many as 100,000, were deported to the Stutthof camp. The prisoners were mainly non-Jewish Poles. There were also Polish Jews from Warsaw and Bialystok, and Jews from forced-labor camps in the occupied Baltic states, which the Germans evacuated in 1944 as Soviet forces approached.

Describes conditions in the Stutthof concentration camp
Personal stories

Conditions in the camp were brutal. Many prisoners died in typhus epidemics that swept the camp in the winter of 1942 and again in 1944. Those whom the SS guards judged too weak or sick to work were gassed in the camp's small gas chamber. Gassing with Zyklon B gas began in June 1944. Camp doctors also killed sick or injured prisoners in the infirmary with lethal injections. More than 60,000 people died in the camp.

http://www.ushmm.org/wlc/article.php?lang=en&ModuleId=10005197&printing=yes 26/02/2005

Stutthof
1939 – 1945
View timeline

STUTTHOF: FORCED LABOR AND SUBCAMPS

The Germans used Stutthof prisoners as forced laborers. Some prisoners worked in SS-owned businesses such as the German Equipment Works (DAW), located near the camp. Others labored in local brickyards, in private industrial enterprises, in agriculture, or in the camp's own workshops. In 1944, as forced labor by concentration camp prisoners became increasingly important in armaments production, a Focke-Wulff airplane factory was constructed at Stutthof. Eventually, the Stutthof camp system became a vast network of forced-labor camps; 105 Stutthof subcamps were established throughout northern and central Poland. The major subcamps were Thorn and Elbing.

STUTTHOF: DEATH MARCHES AND EVACUATIONS

The evacuation of prisoners from the Stutthof camp system in northern Poland began in January 1945. When the final evacuation began, there were nearly 50,000 prisoners, the overwhelming majority of them Jews, in the Stutthof camp system. About 5,000 prisoners from Stutthof subcamps were marched to the Baltic Sea coast, forced into the water, and machine gunned. The rest of the prisoners were marched in the direction of Lauenburg in eastern Germany. They were cut off by advancing Soviet forces. The Germans forced the surviving prisoners back to Stutthof. Marching in severe winter conditions and treated brutally by SS guards, thousands died during the march.

In late April 1945, the remaining prisoners were removed from Stutthof by sea, since Stutthof was completely encircled by Soviet forces. Again, hundreds of prisoners were forced into the sea and shot. Over 4,000 were sent by small boat to Germany, some to the Neuengamme concentration camp near Hamburg, and some to camps along the Baltic coast. Many drowned along the way. Shortly before the German surrender, some prisoners were transferred to Malmo, Sweden, and released to the care of that neutral country. It has been estimated that over 25,000 prisoners, one in two, died during the evacuation from Stutthof and its subcamps.

Soviet forces liberated Stutthof on May 9, 1945, and liberated about 100 prisoners who had managed to hide during the final evacuation of the camp.

Related Links

Teaching about the Holocaust--ONLINE WORKSHOP, personal testimony

Related Articles

Nazi Camps

UNITED STATES HOLOCAUST MEMORIAL MUSEUM

Steven Springfield

Describes conditions in the Stutthof concentration camp [1990 interview]
(Full transcript follows biography)
Born Riga, Latvia
1923

The Germans occupied Riga in 1941, and confined the Jews to a ghetto. In late 1941, about 28,000 Jews from the ghetto were massacred at the Rumbula forest, near Riga. Steven and his brother were sent to a small ghetto for able-bodied men. In 1943 Steven was deported to the Kaiserwald camp and sent to a nearby work camp. In 1944 he was transferred to Stutthof and forced to work in a shipbuilding firm. In 1945, Steven and his brother survived a death march and were liberated by Soviet forces.

United States Holocaust Memorial Museum - Collections

Full transcript
After we arrived in Danzig, when we heard that we were going to Stutthof, we were devastated because Stutthof was a camp which was very well known as one of the worst. There was no food. Was a lot of brutality, a lot of killings and hardly anybody esc...got out... got out of Stutthof, so the three of us, my brother, my father and I, went to Stutthof and spent several weeks there. The conditions in Stutthof were beyond any description. People were dying left and right from hunger. People woke up in the morning, next to you people were dead, emaciated. And the condition was deteriorating by the day because the tide of the war had turned and as bad as it was before, now the Germans were letting their anger out on the few remaining Jews because they were...they were...it was clear to them by this time they were losing the war. A few weeks after we arrived in Stutthof, we were all lined up one day and a German officer said they are looking for volunteers to work in a German shipbuilding firm in Danzig called Schichau-Werft. My brother and I and my father volunteered, but as my father was going across to join us, the German officer noticed that he was invalid--he was dragging a leg as a result of scarlet fever which he had in his youth. The minute he noticed that he says, "You cannot go. Back." My brother and I started pleading, "It's our father. We have to go together." Just to spite, he says, "You're going and he's staying here." And no matter how much we begged and no matter how much we pleaded and cried, it did not help. We were kicked and beaten and forced to leave my father. It was clear to my brother and myself that the minute my...my father would be left in Stutthof he would be doomed. And we were...we were absolutely heart-broken to leave him there, because we knew it was going to be the end. But we were forced to do it and that's how we left Stutthof.

Karl – Stern by name and stern by nature

Karl stayed at home until late 1939. It was then that Adolph and Sarah finally succumbed to the problems of being Jewish in a small village. They had both been badly beaten several times, and were the last Jews in Gladenbach. He took his lead from his father, who was Stern by name and by nature too. He had shown this side of himself frequently to the girls, and even though Selma was a little older than him, he was the same with her. He still played the part of a disapproving big brother to them.

Karl had registered to take the name Israel in February 1939, as had his parents and Dora, in line with the Nazi requirements. Prior to this he had, along with the others, applied for and acquired an identity card from the police, which had to be shown on demand to anyone. He was known to the Gestapo, and in June 1939, was arrested and sent to a 'forced labour concentration camp'. A year later, he was bought out by good friends, with the assurance that he would emigrate as soon as was humanly possible, even though his passport had been stamped with a large red 'J'.

Karl's name change document

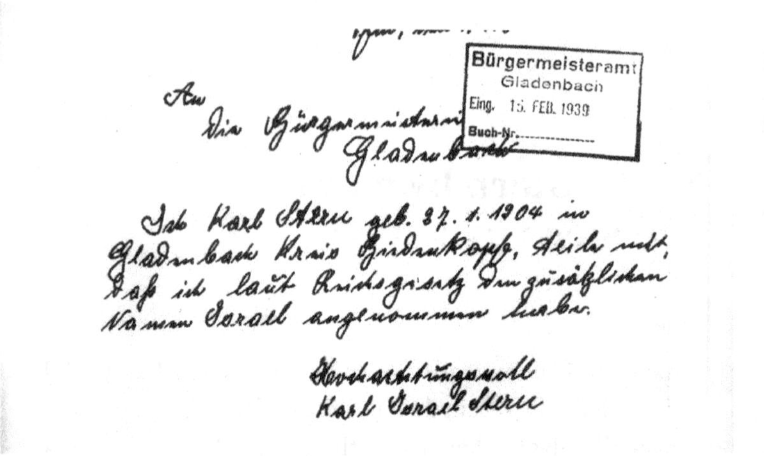

Bürgermeisteramt
Gladenbach
Eing. 15. FEB. 1939
Buch-Nr. ....

An
die Bürgermeisterei
Gladenbach

Ich Karl Stern geb. 27.1.1904 in Gladenbach Kreis Biedenkopf, teile mit, daß ich laut Reichsgesetz den zusätzlichen Namen Israel angenommen habe.

Hochachtungsvoll
Karl Israel Stern

They all (Adolph, Sarah and Karl) moved to Frankfurt, hoping to get lost in the big city. Karl was still treated by his parents as the prodigal son, and his father gave him money, saying the equivalent of 'go west young man!' By this time Karl was 36 years old. In July of 1940 he set off for America, but was to go the long way round via Moscow, Shang-hai and Japan. The journey was to take him more than halfway around the world.

Adolph and Sarah moved in with Selma. Klara had left by then on 31st December 1938, and Dora had married in the meantime, never returning to Frankfurt. She had emigrated with her husband to the Dominican Republic in 1940, where Ernst her husband, hoped to use his knowledge and skills. In October 1938, Klara had told Karl that she was pregnant to her lover, but he gave her a very negative response, just when she was looking for something positive in her life. So she left Germany in December of 1938, almost six months pregnant.

Karl said some awful things to her, and essentially did not want to know. Her parents never knew about the baby.

Karl discovered that the only way out of Nazi Germany was to bribe his way out and fly to Moscow. He had to obtain all kinds of paperwork, including a pass for his luggage. In addition to one change of clothes, nightwear and shoes, as a Jew, Karl was allowed a prayer book, a travel blanket and the silverware Jews were permitted to keep, which was two each of knives, forks, spoons and small spoons, plus two small silver bowls. In addition, he took with him enough food for six days' journey. In reality the long journey took him more than one month. On the morning of 22nd July 1940, Karl found himself in Yokohama after travelling by plane, train and boat, many thousands of miles. He discovered he had been assigned a cabin on the ' Hikawa Maru' sailing from Yokahama to Seattle in the United States of America. This ship was a Japanese liner requisitioned to bring home Japanese prisoners of war. His cabin number was 303 and he was to share with Dr. Neumann, Mr. Jacks and Ernst Steifel. Ernst Steifel wrote a personal diary of his travels, (included at the end of this chapter) and other than the fact of him travelling from Germany to Moscow by train, an incredible journey in itself, Karl got on a plane and met the others in Moscow. Karl finally reached American soil on August 3rd 1940, but far from settling in Seattle (this was where the ship docked) he went on to live in Chicago, and only settled in Seattle in 1943. During his time in Chicago, he met and married Gertrude, who was already pregnant, and later had a son who she named Isaac. Karl became more Jewish than an Orthodox Jew, and lived by his religious beliefs and customs, living until he was 86 and still married to Gertrude. Dora never liked her and said that her pregnancy, and later birth of a son, was to someone else!

She was convinced that Stan did not belong to Karl, even though he had the name Stern. I think that is something we will never know.

Ernst Steifel discovered that he would share the journey overland (via Perm, Sverdlovsk, Omsk, Novosibbirsk, Krasnoyarsk, Lake Baikal, Chita, Otpor, Manchuria, Harbin, Hsingknig, Korea, Fusan), and sea, in the same company as one Karl Stern, amongst others, sharing a cabin on the Hikawa Maru from Yokohama to Vancouver. This piece of memoir was written by him, but I guess it could have been written by Karl, at least from Moscow to Yokohama. Ernst Steifel travelled from Frankfurt by train and had an awful journey on 2nd July 1940. He retells the traumas of his journey in the first few pages of his unpublished work. He met Karl in Moscow on Sunday 7th July, Karl having flown to Moscow from Frankfurt. I think maybe Karl did not have as many problems with border controls as Ernst. It cannot have been easy, but however much he suffered, he cannot possibly have suffered as Selma did, his older sister.

During the course of copying this piece of writing out, I have to admit I found it somewhat boring and missed out many pages of what I thought was trivia. Ernst writes in great detail, which I felt that I and other readers did not need to know, so you will have to forgive me if you wanted to know more. In complaining about the conditions on his journey, my strong impression is that he hung onto his German attitudes and expectations, talking about cleanliness and fatty food, which by comparison would be the last things on Selma's mind.

In order to get his luggage through the many border controls from Frankfurt to Moscow, Ernst had to obtain a Clearance Certificate, as the one he had was considered to be too old, being issued in March of that year. He was allowed to take with him one small suitcase. He talks of having 'the clothes on his back' plus other clothes. One dark suit, one light suit, one summer pullover, one pair pants, one summer overcoat, six pairs socks, eleven handkerchiefs, two neckties, six shirts, three sets of underwear, one pair pyjamas, one pair gym shoes, one belt, three pairs of shoes and one coverall. Presumably this list included all the clothes he was wearing. He was also allowed to take the silverware which Jews were permitted to keep, ie. two each silver spoons, forks, knives, small spoons, two silver bowls, toilet articles, two towels, one travel blanket, one prayer book and other very small items, in addition to food to last the journey. Ernst went from Frankfurt to Hamburg and talks of reaching Hamburg in an air raid, and he wrote that he had $3.80 and 11.70 Reichsmark. This was later taken away from him, leaving him the $3.80 (as this was the equivalent of 10 Marks German money) after he had bought his tickets which would take him over land and sea to reach America. He went halfway around the world to get there, and this in itself must have been an epic journey.

Ernst lists all the travellers by name who he met from Germany to America, plus he attempted to say where in America they were heading if he knew, and what they did to survive. After staying in a hotel in Moscow, he set off for America via the trans-Siberian railway.

The Trip – Travel overland Moscow to Yokohama – by Ernst Steifel

Sometime between 3:00 and 4:00p.m., on Sunday July 7th 1940 our group was taken by bus from the Hotel Metropole to the Moscow Yarosel railroad station. From this particular station trains were going East, it was a very primitive station and did not have the European features of the Byelorussian station. I do not know how our luggage was transported but it got there. The members of our group who had checked in luggage form Berlin to Moscow had a surprise in store. Their luggage did not arrive with them in Moscow. It was delayed en route and I do not know what happened to it. These people did not have any clothes or belongings for the long trip ahead.

About 4:30p.m the Trans-Siberian Express appeared. I was assigned to car no. 3, bed 17. Since second-class had been sold out I was given third-class accommodation. In my compartment were four men, a Dane, Mr. Munk who was travelling to Beijing (I suspected he was a fifth columnist), a Russian who could speak no German and one Karl Stern who was a German in the same predicament as me. The Trans-Siberian Express was not a luxury train. There were no Pullman cars, just primitive sleepers which were not very clean. The dining car was also dirty and not very appealing. I found only two decent cars in this ten car train, one was occupied by a Japanese Trade delegation and the other was first-class only. On time, at 5:00p.m.the train left the station in the direction of Siberia.

All cars of the train were equipped with loud speakers and they broadcast either recorded music or radio music and also the news. I noted that with exception of Beethoven's Fifth Symphony on the first day and Wagner on the third day, the music was awful. At midnight on the first night of our trip, they played 'Internationale' broadcast from Moscow.

Third-class consisted of a wooden bench with an upper bunk, also made of wood and fitted with a thin mattress. It was not particularly comfortable but had to do. For the most part I did not stay in my compartment during the day; I spent my time in other compartments talking with other travellers. I used my compartment mostly for sleeping and did not exchange many words with Mr. Munk and the Dane and had no communication with the Russian soldier. On the other hand I often talked to the German Jew who turned out to be going to America to be with friends.

The train did not set any speed records and I noted at the time that it was travelling at about the same speed as a local German train and it also shook quite a bit. I was happy when the train made a stop at a station usually for twenty minutes. I found I could stretch there and obtain hot water from which I brewed tea. The water on the train was undrinkable. The toilet facilities were primitive to say the least, especially in third-class and often water was not available. During a stop at a station the train's toilets which also contained a washbasin were locked. The dining car seemed especially bumpy. The food was good but fatty and all the travellers, including myself, suffered from stomach trouble. Those travelling were assigned to one of three different shifts for meals: in the mornings at 8, 9 and 10a.m. At the middle of the day at 1, 2 or 3p.m. and in the evening at 8, 9 or 10 p.m., I was in the last group. Breakfast was on time, lunch I eat at 4p.m. and I generally completed dinner at around midnight. Dessert usually consisted of old, dried fruit which was quite hard. The service was very slow and not too good. The last few days I lost patience and joined the first or second group as I did not want to eat so late. To get our meals we had to surrender the coupons which we had received with the railroad tickets. If we had a special request, we had to ask for it about ten times and maybe or maybe not get it.

The days on the Trans-Siberian Express were very boring. There was a representative of Intourist travel agency on board, he spoke German and I talked to him often. He was, I thought, somewhat narrow minded. The further East the train travelled the worse the stations became. Every night we set the clocks ahead one hour except for the last night. The stations had two clocks, one showing Moscow tome and one showing local time.

Monday July 8th 1940 – It was an especially hot day and we suffered from the heat. The train seemed to be of World War One vintage and did not have any air conditioning. Early on Tuesday, July 9th at 1 a.m. the train arrived in Perm (later known as Molotov) apparently a beautiful city fully lit and a pleasure to look at. The same day at around 11a.m. we went through Sverdlovsk. Early in the morning on Wednesday July 10th we crossed the border between European and Asian Russia. I honoured this occasion by sleeping through it. That same morning at 6a.m. the train passed through Omsk and at 4:30p.m. through Novosibirsk. The landscape in Siberia was dull, every so often one could see a hut and an outhouse and they looked kind of miserable. With the exception of the large cities the scenery was mainly the Steppes. It seemed to be hot all the time except for the region around Lake Baikal. On Thursday July 11th in the early morning, the train stopped at Krasnoyarsk and on Friday afternoon (12th) our trip took us to Irkutsk and through the most scenic parts of of Siberia.

The train travelled for almost 200 miles along the lake and Angara River. I was impressed by the mountains and the beautiful surroundings. The lake contained icebergs and is supposedly 5,700 feet deep. I only saw part of it because that Friday my stomach started to bother me.

Friday night and Shabbat morning religious services were held in one of the second-class compartments. There was just enough room in the crowded compartment for the ten men required for a Minyan prayer service. In addition to the ten men in the compartment, one man stood outside to make sure that the rest of us did not get into trouble in Godless Russia. Saturday, July 13th at 2p.m. saw the train stopped in Chita and for the first time in my life, I saw Mongolians who came to the train. The

Russian soldier and the Russian Jew who was teaching Atheism, left the train.

A peasant woman with 6 children came into my compartment. They all occupied one bed – how they did it I don't know. The stench they gave off was horrible and I could not stand it. I spent much of my time in other compartments and after a while the woman and her children left the train and I went back to my compartment.

We became very excited as we approached the Manchurian border. Rumours abounded as to the time of our arrival at the border in Otpor; at one time we were told that it would be 3a.m. and then 7a.m. was mentioned. We all had extra dining car coupons and mindful that we had to provide food for the trip to Manchuli, we exchanged these coupons for whatever food we could get. The Russians took advantage of us and we did not get as much food as we were entitled to. I surrendered coupons for six meals and received 200 grams of butter and 400 grams each of cheese and sausage. I also got some bread. Around midnight on Saturday night our passports were returned. They had been taken from us when we had entered the Trans-Siberian Express train. I commented at the time that the Russians did not trust us.

At 6a.m. on Sunday July 13th we arrived at the border station of Otpor and the train was seven hours late. For an hour prior to our arrival the curtains at the windows had to be closed so that we could not see any of the military fortifications. Our luggage was brought to the custom house and everything was examined very thoroughly. The Russians were interested in everything anyone had written and this and all photographs were examined very closely. All blank paper, including toilet paper, was looked through. We had to count our foreign currency to the officials and we were again told that we could not export any Russian roubles. The border officials also asked us about pistols, guns, cameras and typewriters, none of which I had. One couple were typing a report whilst travelling on the train and everyone who went by their compartment could see that. Their report never left Russia and was confiscated at the border. For that reason I did not write down my impressions of the trip until I was onboard the Hikawa Maru ship about ten days later.

Having gone through a Russian border control at Bigosowo already, I knew the game. For that reason I stuck my most important papers, possessions and my prayer book in my coat pocket and the Russians never looked at that. The border control took a great amount of time and the train only left Otpor at 10:30a.m., to arrive at the Manchurian border town of Manchuli at 11:00a.m. What a difference between Russia and Manchuria! As we arrived at the destination of the train in Manchuli, we had to go to the customs house at the station.

It was quite hot and flies were buzzing everywhere. What a hustle and bustle in comparison to the slow and phlegmatic Russians. First we had to fill out a form to declare our foreign currency (I still have a copy of this form). On it I gave my German address, listed my occupation as 'apprentice' said I started the trip in Frankfurt and that my final destination was Brooklyn, New York, U.S.A. I also declared I had $3.80 in US currency. There is a stamp in Japanese on the form and I do not know what it says.

We then opened our luggage and once again the border control guards rummaged through the contents. Then I went to passport control and was asked to come to another room. I could not find my passport! I found it at last and was again questioned. I was not only asked about my occupation but age, origin and to where and whom I was going in America. I told them I was going to my cousin's but somehow they were unable to comprehend the word 'cousin.'

Once this was completed, some of the men travelling with the group wired the Jewish community in Harbin requesting money to pay for the overnight stay in Manchuli. We were informed that the train to Harbin and east of there was full and that we had to take the train the next day. Like gypsies, exhausted, harassed and suffering from the heat we sat at the roadside of the station in Manchuli. Then at 3:30p.m., the local police told us to move on and leave the station within half an hour. With great effort I found a hotel in Manchuli. A group of us stayed at the Hotel Tamaja, a Japanese hotel with all the accommodations Japanese style. In the rooms were large platforms and small tables and pillows on the floor. At night, mats, pillows and quilts were put on the platform. I washed myself thoroughly, a necessary task after all the dirt on the Trans-Siberian Express, then I walked through the village of Manchuli which had 3,000 inhabitants. As I walked I was conscious of people looking at me, this strange European.

Manchuria and especially Manchuli, impressed me. The cleanliness and the rush and particularly the activities of the Japanese. The difference between Russia and Manchuria was like night and day, the only thing was the disturbance of all the flies. At the Japanese Tourist Bureau there was a billboard for Bad Nauheim, Germany and next to it one for Harbin. Back in the hotel I found a copy of a German Foreign Office White Paper. They had rationing in Manchuria including cigarettes. Our dinner in the hotel consisted of the food which I had brought from the train. There were twenty of us and we shared our food. We ordered three samovers full of tea and drank it all being as we were very thirsty. After dinner we took a walk through the village but we were told by the police there was a curfew for us and to get back to the hotel. This was explained as a 'defence measure.'

Monday morning, July 14th the group had breakfast together and drank tea again. Breakfast completed I was told that the

Japanese Tourist Board had some money for me. I went there and was handed the following telegram from Harbin:

Ernst Steifel, c/o Japan Tourist Bureau, Manchouli,
received from the Central Bank Yen 210.70 include board money
Specie Bank

The telegram had a stamp with the date 15th July 1940 Manchouli, MTT Co.

A Jew from the village went with me to the bank and after identifying myself, I received the Yen 210.70. This was the $50 which my brother Siegfried had sent me for the trip and included money for on board ship. As the money was Yen it was probably not exchangeable for dollars. I now was a rich person since no one in the group had any money aside from the $3.80 they had been allowed to take out of Germany. With that money I paid every one's bill at the hotel and I was paid, by them, the equivalent in US dollars. We never did receive any money from the Jewish community in Harbin.

I was so lucky as all along the way I had exchanged my Yen for dollars and managed to arrive in Seattle with $50 US in currency. Now, in retrospect, I ask myself whether I needed that much cash because at that time $50 was not easy to come by for an immigrant. Siegfried had to borrow these funds, which I later paid back. I did not know that I would get money back from the rail road, since sleepers were not available between Manchuli and Yokohama.

I probably could have made it without the $50 but barely. I could not have been able to purchase some much needed extra clothes etc., in Japan and on the boat. I would also not have had the luxury of sending a telegram to my parents from Yokohama to Germany. In Manchuli I purchased a loaf of bread, a piece of *soap (the German soap was very poor since the start of the war). I also bought two chocolate bars, a packet of tea and a comb all for Yen 3.70. At that time there were 4.20.Yen to the US dollar.*

Something disagreeable happened in Manchouli. One of the group went into a store and gave the merchant $1 and requested the exchange of Yen 5 even though the official rate was Yen 4.20. The merchant exchanged the dollar for the Yen requested but reported this to the passport office. When I got to the office, the unofficial leader of the group who was a physician and a lawyer in the group were there and explained the situation. I showed the official telegram I had received and the person was then on the telephone for quite some time. He spoke Japanese so I did not understand a single word. When he spoke, he told us that this time we would get a warning and if it happened again we would either be sent to jail or returned to Russia.

After that I left the hotel and went to the railroad station. The official from the Japanese Tourist Board handed us the tickets to Yokohama. There were no sleepers to Harbin for single men and I was paid Yen 4.50 back. This was the first money that I had 'earned' outside of Germany. The train left the station at 12.40p.mp. During the first hour the blinds were pulled down so we could not see out. Our second-class compartment was full of Manchurian soldiers. When they found out we came from Germany they called us 'our friends'. I noted that the second-class compartments looked like German ones and were very clean and comfortable.

What a difference between Russia and Japanese occupied Manchuria. The train and railroad were clean, the train had ventilation and the dining car was appetising. The countryside looked very attractive and one could see this was a much richer country. The Japanese were well dressed and this was the first time I had seen ladies in kimonos. The toilet facilities were very good and sanitary and when a train was about to leave a station they rang a bell, just like the bells in school. The train arrived in Harbin at 2.20p.m. on the 16th July 1940. Prior to arrival we once again had to surrender our passports. At the station, several gentlemen from the Jewish community greeted us. Our luggage was stored in the waiting room and we went to the passport agency to answer all kinds of questions.

It was raining very hard in Harbin when we arrived. After completion of formalities we were taken by bus to the Jewish community building. A city tour was thought about but because it was raining so heavy, it was cancelled. Whatever little we saw of Harbin indicated that it was both a Russian and Chinese city as signs were generally in both languages. We met some individuals who lived for the most part in Shang-Hai but left that city to escape the heat for the summer. Later on in Harbin, we enjoyed a good evening meal. After food rationing in Germany and the food on the train from Russia, anything decent looked good to me. My notes show that I ate two portions. We were taken by bus again back to the railway station, again for passport control. Those who had larger luggage were asked to send it in the baggage car to Yokohama. I did not check in anything since I had only the one suitcase.

Those who checked in their luggage ended up in Kobe for two days and did not get thei luggage until we reached Yokohama. In other places our luggage was taken in and out of the train, through windows, stacked somewhere until people were told to pick out their own and claim it back.

The next train was crowded and no sleepers were available. Right on time the train left the station on July 17th and arrived in time in the capital city of Manchuria. We had more than one hour to kill and I walked out of the station to look around. First I got a shoe shine then I bought a can of juice, I had spent less than 1 Yen. I walked by a butcher who displayed his wares on an outdoor table in front of the railroad station. Flies buzzed over all the raw meat and the whole display did not look very appetising. Despite it being early in the morning, it was quite hot. Other food was handled in a similar manner and I did not get a good impression of the city.

The train arrived at Fusan an hour and quarter late and because of that we had missed the boat! We stored our luggage at the railroad station and since it was raining heavily, went into a nearby restaurant and ordered lunch. The food was very cheap and I had a good meal for less than 50 cents. The rain stopped and I decided to have a look at Fusan. It was a small fishing village and again the locals looked at us as though we had just arrived from Mars. We decided, as it had started to rain again, to get a cup of coffee or tea at the restaurant.

Somewhere in between I got a haircut which I badly needed because it seemed so long since I had left Germany. The barber also shaved me and used all sorts of hot and cold compresses on my face and neck. All this for the equivalent of 15 cents! hours later we were thrown out of the restaurant. We returned to the railway station which was also the boat terminal. We all sat in the waiting room and were stared at by the local people. We were subject to yet another passport inspection and again asked the usual questions of name, occupation, place of origin and where we were going to.

At 9p.m. we went to the pier since we could not board the boat for another half an hour.

I had a second-class ticket and sleeping was Japanese style i.e. there was one large sleeping room for about 200 people with large platforms with mats and very hard pillows. On board this boat I was able to exchange my Manchurian and Korean coins for Japanese currency. People brought our luggage and the customs officials waved us on; for the first time we did not have to open the suitcases. My suitcase was handled by throwing it at me and when opened, I discovered that two bottles of eau-de-cologne were broken and the contents spilled all over my belongings. In spite of everything – I slept well.

Friday 19th July and it was 6:00a.m. I found the most beautiful Japanese scenery to look at and the weather was sunny. Once again I had to surrender my passport and fill out forms. As the boat arrived in Shimonoseki, the Japanese passport control officers came onto the boat and stamped my passport with 'Permitted to Transit'. Now I was in Japan and I boarded a train for Tokyo. The train ride took us along the Japanese Riviera and it was very beautiful. The dining car was again very clean and quite inexpensive, it was also very hot, about 32c I think.

We were very comfortably seated as the train arrived in Kobe and a few gentlemen from the Jewish community entered the train and told us that we had to get out at Sannomiya station in three minutes. They also informed us that if we didn't have a place to stay in Yokohama, the police would send us away. With great difficulty we got our things together and left the train at the said station at 7:30p.m. The leader of the delegation from Kobe was a former Jewish lawyer from Frankfurt and a friend of my brother's. He told me that I was the first person from Frankfurt that travelled through Kobe. In Kobe we stayed at a nearby house which the committee had rented for transients. Once we arrived there we had a good meal then we gave our passports and tickets to one of the gentlemen who took the night train to Yokohama to make sure that our transpacific passages were in order. The next day (July 20th) I helped to fetch breakfast from the Jewish community house, otherwise it was too hot to do anything. We spent a pleasant day and at 5:00p.m. and had our smallpox immunization at the office of a physician. The next day was a hot one too and I went shopping and bought some new clothes, cleaned my room and ate an agreeable dinner.

Japanese children appeared to be very well behaved as they hardly cried even when they were in pain. Traffic in Japan is on the left the same as in England and I saw billboards with swastika and the Japanese and Italian flags together. The train to Yokohama left at 8 p.m. and was clean and modern, it was also not very full and I was able to sleep most of the way. Monday morning early, the train arrived in Yokohama, the destination of our land travel. There were several gentlemen from the Jewish community to meet us and we were taken to get straight on the Hikawa Maku. Our luggage also was taken to the boat.

I found out and was glad that I was assigned to cabin 303 along with Dr. Neumann, Mr. Karl Stern (who later operated a tailor shop in Seattle) and Mr. Jacks. We filled out some forms with personal information and surrendered our passports yet again. We also found that our passage had not been paid for and it was only due to the generosity of a well to do Jewish individual, who kindly advanced the funds for our passage, that we were able to leave that afternoon for America.

The Sea Journey

I do not have many notes about travelling on the boat to America but safe to say the Hikawa Maru was not the most modern but fairly comfortable. The journey was quite boring after all the train travel there was not much to do and the sea was so calm, nobody was even sea sick. I remember it was very cold on deck and in our third-class cabin there were eight bunks. As there were only four of us this was fine, however, I did not spend much time in there anyway. The third class dining room was very simple and we sat along long tables. There were two sittings, one for Asians and one for Europeans. The food was good and plentiful and was served to us, European style. There was no selection and we ate what we were given. I ate well on board. I passed the time, sitting around, walking on deck and meeting with new friends from first-class. On July 26th there was broadcast this message on board: Since we cross the 180th meridian at about 2:30a.m. tomorrow, Saturday will be repeated. Thus we had Saturday twice but it was now 27th July. On the first of these Saturdays we had religious services and we barely had a Minyan. As we travelled east we constantly our clocks ahead by 30 minutes, until July 30th this being a total of six hours. Each day we mimeographed a newspaper and this was the first 'free' and uncensored news I had read in a long time. I bought some things and clothes on board and also had another haircut. On August 1st we heard that the boat would dock in Vancouver the next day and that medical inspection would be held for all passengers soon after arrival. Passengers were requested to assemble in the dining room with their vaccination and inoculation certificates. In addition there was a passport inspection. Because I was German and Canada was at present at war with Germany, I was not allowed to get off the boat in Vancouver. This was all then repeated by the US Immigration officer. First he reviewed the papers of those allowed off the boat in Vancouver and then he looked at ours. He called us 'enemy aliens' and treated us as such. He worked all day on reviewing all documents. In addition to the visa in my passport I had an Immigrant Identification Card plus some more papers including my affidavit of support. It turned out that each of the three United States Consulates in Germany, handled things in a different way. Berlin gave the immigrant complete copies of the affidavit, Stuttgart just a summary and Hamburg gave nothing. The final decision as of whether i was allowed in to the U.S.A. lay with this man who was checking my papers. He had no trouble with the people from Berlin and seemed to be satisfied with the Stuttgart summary but struggled with the papers from Hamburg. In some cases he almost decided that he would not admit those from Hamburg. I remember one man saying he was a leading surgeon and not just anybody but it made no difference. The matter was only solved after a certain Jewish businessman from Seattle gave another affidavit of support for all those poor people.

Whilst in Vancouver I received a letter from my brother, welcoming me to America and giving me much needed advice of what to do. He had sent me $35 (all he could raise) and said that this money and whatever I already had, would have to do for a while. He also told me that I would have to stay in Seattle as there was no way he could buy me a train ticket to New York and besides, the job situation would be better in Seattle. He realised that I had brought with me very little from Germany and said he would send me some clothes in return for an answer for which he had enclosed a stamped addressed envelope.

After all this excitement, I went to sleep on Friday night August 2nd for the last time on the Hikawa - Maru. Early in the morning, the boat pulled into the Great Northern Dock, Pier 88, in Seattle. It took some time before our group could get off the boat but the sun was shining and the weather could not have been better. So down the gangplank I went into the hall next to the dock. There was the usual customs check and many Seattle Jewish individuals were on hand to greet us. Ours was the first boat of new immigrants to arrive in Seattle via Russia. I arrived in Seattle with no luggage and the story of my luggage arriving more than six months later is something else to be told but I did not care. The long and arduous journey was over and a new life in America was about to begin. This was to be a new and different chapter of my life.

Klara – who was shy, laughing and childlike.

Klara went to Frankfurt on her 33rd birthday in May, 1938. This was an enormously brave thing for her to do, as she had never been away from home before. Everything had become so difficult in Gladenbach, she felt that she had to leave, what with that and her mother and father keep saying that she would be better off in Frankfurt. It was walkable to the train station from where she lived, so she got the small mountain train that went directly to Frankfurt. Selma met her when she arrived in the city, and explained to Klara that she could not live with her because she lived in lodgings. Klara would have to find lodgings of her own, but she would regularly meet up with both Selma and Dora.

Klara had soon found lodgings in a Jewish household. The son of the woman who owned the house was so handsome, and Klara began to think it would not be so bad, being away from home. Through the coming months, despite the Nazi oppression, Klara became close to the son of the house and in July 1938, she slept with him. In October she told him that she thought she was pregnant, and he was so thrilled that he announced his undying love for her, promising that they would marry just as soon as he could organise it. The political climate was very bad, and they talked about going to England together. It was around this time that Klara told Selma about her pregnancy. Klara had thought that because Selma and she were so close, Selma would be understanding and supportive. She wasn't! In fact, she reacted just like Karl did when Klara told him later.

The beginning of November saw Klara with no other support, both emotionally and financially, than her lover. On the night of 9th November – Kristallnacht (night of the broken glass) occurred. Non-Jews were warned before the wave of nationwide violence, but it came as a complete surprise to Klara and her lover. Any Jews out on the streets were beaten up, and shops had their windows broken and daubed with slogans. Tens of thousands of young Jewish men were arrested, never to be seen again. Presumably they were sent to labour concentration camps. Klara's lover, David's father, was one of these, and she never saw him again.

Her thoughts had been shattered like the broken windows. All Klara could think about in the days after the horrors of Kristallnacht was carrying out her lover's plan to go to England, and make the substance of her dreams a reality. She was dimly aware of people trying to carry on whilst not really feeling a part of it. They had found joy in doing things together and now he was no more. Sometimes, she could not believe there would be a life without him. Selma was not speaking to her, neither was Dora, and she could not possibly tell her parents of her situation. She convinced herself they were too old to take in such monumental news. Klara set about getting all the papers she needed to get out of Germany and go to England. When leaving Germany, the officials took away any existing passport and gave the person a 'Nansenpass'. This was a travel document stating identity but not Nationality. This, in effect, made the holder stateless.

Klara set out on her journey on 30.12.38. She had heard that if you had a sponsor in England it would be much easier to enter the country. So she had written to Dr. Meyer, who she knew had got out of Germany in 1935, and he lived in Harrogate. At this point she did not mention she was pregnant. Dr. Meyer wrote back to her that he would sponsor her. If she could get on a boat, she could come straight to Harrogate when she landed in England. He seemed to know a lot about what was happening, and advised Klara to say that she was a domestic, as this would satisfy English officials. This, for a middle class German woman, was terrible. Klara was considered to be really lucky to have got a place on the boat, as there were very long waiting lists to enter another country, so she should be grateful. It was only late in 1938 that Britain opened its doors to 'domestics'. Every letter leaving Germany was opened and censored. If the letter contained anything slightly suspicious or what was considered to be against the state, the writer was traced, arrested and sent to a concentration camp. Klara was so happy and Dr. Meyer's letter seemed to give her the courage she needed. She had heard of 'Kinder transport' and managed to convince the powers that be that she would be an asset to these children during their long journey. To her delight she was offered a place on the boat that sailed on 31.12.1938. She was allowed to take with her very little money, one change of clothes and one set of cutlery. Married women were allowed to keep their wedding ring. Klara went directly from Hamburg to Harwich, having arrived in England later that day. It had been a very rough crossing and as Klara was very sick, she was no use to the children. In fact it depressed her knowing that all these children would never see their parents or their homeland again. She was one of them, although by this time, she was 34.

Klara walked off the boat feeling really bad, and was met by a Jewish lady who worked for the Refugee Children's Movement. She was immediately handed over to the German Jewish Aid Committee. A female worker gave her a white apron and told her to wear a plain dress. Klara was also given the same leaflet which was given to all Germans on arrival in England. It was called 'Whilst you are in England.' In essence it said: Do not speak German whilst in England, do not be noisy or speak in a loud voice and do not dress precociously. There were many other do's and don'ts contained within this pamphlet, and it was written in English as well as German. Goodness knows what Klara thought and felt on reading the pamphlet, she couldn't possibly have felt welcome, and speaking not a word of English only made it worse.

The following words were taken and typed out (by me) from the original social work case notes, kept by the German Jewish Aid Committee:-

Klara Stern	No. 19071
Date of birth:	16.05.1905
Arrived in England	31.12.38.
05.04.39.	Harwich direct from Germany. Entered with visa to work as a domestic for Dr. Meyer, 7 York Road, Harrogate. Visa granted 28.12.38. Was sent here by Leeds Committee as is pregnant.
07.04.39.	Mrs Motel says Jewish Maternity Home full up.
08.04.39.	Mrs. R.M. Cohen granted 25/- and £2. 8. 0.

07.07.39	Luggage to be collected and stored by Pall Mall as mentioned by Mrs. Scherab.
11.07.39.	Asked Miss Meyerhof to visit her at St Pancras Hospital as requested by the Matron of St Pancras.
19.07.39.	Called here today saying that she had been discharged from the hospital 18.07.39. Asked for a doctor. Refused. Told her to go re: a post to see Mrs. Price on Mrs. Scherab's suggestion???????
26.07.39.	Dress, 1 vest, 1 knicker, 2 stockings given.
31.07.39.	To find very cheap accommodation at our expense. 20 shillings a week.
11.08.39.	Mrs. Patel, 34 Hilldrop Crescent, Brecknock Road, N.7. Cheque paid for two weeks board and lodging £2.10.0.
14.08.39.	Mrs. Patel paid for a further week at 25/- full board on \mrs. Scherab's instructions.
18.08.39.	£3.15.0. paid for baby.
23.08.39.	Placed at Atkinson's Hostel – Committee's expense (Mrs. Scherab's instructions) pending finding a post.
24.08.39.	Pocket money and fare to Bedford 7/-
28.02.39.	Cheque to Mrs. Patel for 1 weeks board and lodging. 14th – 24th August £1.5 shillings

31.08.39.	Maintenance paid £3. 10 shillings
17.10.39.	Luggage bill 9/9
07.11.39.	For child 1.9. – 29.9.39. Maintenance (12/6 weekly) £2.10shillings. Acceptance must be got to have child taken away.
24.11.39.	L.C.C. Hospital 7.7. – 18.&.39. £1.30 shillings.
30.11.39.	Hospital fees - £6.5 shillings.
11.12.39.	Fever S. (baby to remain at All Saints Nursery see notes 1.12.39
20.12.39.	Bill luggage 8/9.
31.01.40.	Referred case to Domestic Department. Pocket money 1/6.
13.02.40.	Referred All Saints Nursery to D.B. re David.
21.02.40.	All Saints Nursery College maintenance for child from 5.1.40. – 31.1.40. Refer to D.D. £2.9s 6d
05.03.40.	For baby 2 vests, shoes, 2 socks, pullover, dress.
24.01.40.	Luggage 1/3d
23.05.40.	Shoes, boy suit.
03.07.40.	????? to correct address at camp. 2 dresses.
29.09.40.	Paid to L.M.S. for transport of luggage 10/-
October 1940	Interned at Manchester House, Rushen Internment Camp, Port Erin, Isle of Man.
22.11.40.	IT+H sent to Isle of Man. Sender paid.

22.01.41.	L.M.S. forwarding cheque for luggage to I.O.M. 8/2d
21.07.42.	David Stern will go to Mrs. Bates, 34 Queen's Road, Richmond at 18 shillings per week on release from Internment.
05.08.42.	David due to arrive today and proceed to Richmond tomorrow.
01.09.42.	Regional Office state that she would not obtain permission to work with Lyon's. It would have to be essential work such as in a food factory etc. She should register with the Island Exchange.
25.09.42.	David visited by Miss Smith and Mrs. Josse – reports on file.
24.10.42.	Fees in future increased to 25 shillings. Sanction given by Finance and Central Office.
09.12.42.	Mother on release from Internment Camp to stay for one night here at B.H. Has job and rooms to go to next day. Mrs. Markey informed.
11.12.42.	Very good welfare report on David – see file.
07.01.43.	Arrived last night. To see A.B. re. Emergency money and fares to Moulden and money for 1st week. 11 Stanley Avenue, New Moulden, Surrey. To work with Messrs. Senior and Co Ltd., Raynes Park, SW20 as a factory hand. Mrs. Stern will go to see David tomorrow afternoon.

Signed A.B. form (Provincial Care) copy in file.

25.01.43. Has started work, wages £2.15 shillings per week. Asking for a clothing grant.

01.02.43. I saw woman when she called at B.H. on Saturday morning. I have sent report of interview to Miss Fellman as she is dealing with the case.

02.02.43. Calling here having cut in her hand. Outpatient of \nelson Hospital. We phoned Med. Sup. Who informed us she is unfit to work for a short time only having had three stitches in her right hand. She has to see them again on Thursday. We persuaded her to return to her lodgings and not to move. Transfer to Miss Fellman.

10.02.43. At the request of Miss Fellman we took her to our Holmefield Hostel, 14 Belsize Square, N.W.3. as from tomorrow until fit for work again after her accident. Claimed 'Workman's Compensation'. Has about 30 shillings savings so will refund her claim.

12.02.43. This very excitable lady, after her long internment apprears to have no clothes left. We have no luggage of hers and after explaining this to Miss Fellman, it was decided that we grant her the most necessary articles of clothing in spite of the fact that she is working. She went away calmed and happy.

12.02.43. The hospital has said she is fit for work as from????

18.02.43. Will work in a different department of the sauce factory. (Seniors and Co. Ltd) Manager will send us an address to here???

Wimbledon – Kingston L.E. did not grant her release but think that transfer to another department will make it easier for her. She will return to Moulden 17.02.43.

15.02.43. Signed AB form again (Provincial Case/Care) Miss Wheeler (Hanover House) phoned manager of Senior and Co. They have not got the release form. He found her a room and wants to see her this afternoon. Miss Stern will start with firm again.

17.02.43. Will leave Holmefield today for 307 Kingston Road, S.W.20. She will start work again tomorrow. Received up to now one week's compensation of 27/- but has to pay rent, fares and other expenses until she receives first weeks wages. She has promised to pay the 21/- for six days maintenance in Holmefield Hostel @ 3/6d a day in instalments over the next few weeks.

18.02.43.	Most excitable and very full of complaints. However, she tells me that the stitches are to be taken out of her hand on Monday and she will return to work on Thursday.
20.02.43.	I have arranged with Mrs. Sternthat we will try to have David evacuated to a Jewish Home once she has started her new job and that until then, David will remain in Richmond. Given a coat for David.
21.02.43.	Left Holmefield on 17.02.43.
09.04.43.	Signed AB form again (Provincial Case) Copy in file. Med cert given unfit for work for 14 days.
15.06.43.	Repayment to Holmefield Hostel of £1. 1 shilling.
23.08.43.	Letter from Mrs. Stern redirected from AB sent to Dr. Samson for attention.
25.08.43.	She stayed with Miss Danziger 1st-9th August and missed £4 out of her handbag whilst she went downstairs for dinner. The local police have taken over the case and made all enquiries on the spot.
11.02.44	Informed H.O. that Miss Stern discontinued attendance at Belsize Park to take up factory work. Correspondence in JUS private file.
14.03.44.	Commenced work with Allfor Bakeries N.W.6 as factory hand.

	Wages 1/4d per hour. Obtained permit through??? on P.L.xx
11.04.44.	Ill since 3.4.44. Could not work. To AB
25.04.44.	Signed AB form again (Hostel Case) Copy in file.
02.05.44.	Resumed work with Allfor Bakeries on 01.05.44. AB confirmed.
04.05.44.	Shoe repair as only just started earning. 1 pr. socks earnings 34/6d.
18.05.44.	Miss Stern is anxious for David to have a Jewish upbringing and I have asked Miss Stewart to take him to the Beacon.
28.06.44.	David has gone to the Beacon, taken by Miss Levy. Mrs Bates rang up last week to see if we could find somewhere for him by the weekend as she was ill and had to go away.
30.06.44.	Left Holmefield for 4 Oakfield Road, N.W.11 c/o Mrs Lewis.
11.07.44.	Miss Stewart reports that David has settled in very well at the Beacon. Miss Stern has been given notice by Mrs Lewis as per 16.7.44.
21.08.44.	Dr. Schiff saw woman on 17.8.44. when certificate issued for Labour Exchange – suitable for light domestic work etc.
14.09.44.	Miss Stern is working as a daily domestic and earns 55/- per week. She pays 25/- for a room. She gave us some old clothing and asks whether

she could have a dress and a blouse which I have granted.

23.09.44. Signed AB form again (GOL) Copy in file.

28.09.44. B+B for 30/6d to 4.10.44. – still unfit for work, Moving on 6.10.44. to 135 Sumatra Road, N.W.6. for 15/- a week inc. light and????(could not read)

27.11.44. Woman saw Dr. Schiff when certificate issued for Labour Exchange.

01.02.45. Granted one coat. Miss Stern at the moment earns £2.0.0. per week. She pays 15/- rent plus 2/6d?? as does not belong to an approved society. Dr. Schiff saw woman – report to Dr. Rechwalsky. *There are crossed out notes here but it seems Klara was admitted to a private hospital – psychiatric?????*

17.05.45. We arrange for 2 weeks at 19 Warple Road, Epsom as from 28.05.45. Medical certificate and forms with us. Working as a daily help. Earnings for w/e 25.5. are 42/6d Will pay one weeks rent of 17/6d until w/e 30.5.45. Keeps balance for her living and fares from Epsom. Welfare Dept. Will apply for second week rent, as not yet a member of an approved society. In case she receives H.S.B., she will refund it. To AB

	for hostel application. Landlady – Miss Reimel, money to be sent to 8 Dartmouth Road, N.W.2 Signed AB form again (hostel case) copy in file.
22.05.45.	Accepted estimate RMOH????, has own shoes.
11.06.45.	Dr. Glaser rec. exmp until 18.6.45.
21.06.45.	Left Epsom on 18.6.45. for 236 Willesden Lane, N.W.2. According to Dr. Glaser – fit for work.
12.07.45.	Woman called as in need of dental treatment – does not belong to an approved society. Earns £2.2.6d p.w. on average. Referred to Mr. Orley.
24.07.45.	Accepted estimate from Mr. Orley for dental treatment. £3.10.shillings.
03.09.45.	Called here with another certificate from Dr. Bisilan who recommends convalescence (gastritis and nervous debility) Medical certificate and form with us. Will give up her job as does not think she can do such heavy work. Will get last payment of £2.10. shillings today. Has to keep that money for rent (17/6d) while she is away. We arrange for Epsom on 4.9.45. To AB for hostel application. Signed AB form again. (hostel care)
06.09.45.	Mrs. Glaser informs us that Miss Stern has given up her room against our advice.
04.10.45.	Extended until 9.10.45.

17.10.45.	Extended until 23.10.45.
14.11.45.	Extended until 27.11.45.
06.12.45.	Extended until 29.12.45.
21.01.46.	Extended until 04.02.46.
30.01.46.	Paid 10/- to Mr. Orley for dental treatment. Housing to discuss with Miss Glaser about completing dental treatment started by Mr. Orley.
12.02.46.	Stay at Epsom extended until 25.2.46.
23.02.46.	Working four hours a day as domestic kitchen help. Earnings 10/- a week. Discussed case with Hostel Accounts Dept. Miss Stern is awarded??? earnings??? Permitted to keep 10/- Fares and insurance may be deducted from this. Balance to be paid to Hostel Warden for maintenance.
12.03.46.	Accepted estimate from dentist in Epsom for £6.7.6d
29.04.46.	Left Epsom without warning. Destination unknown.
21.08.46.	Writing to Special Investigations Branch, New Scotland Yard asking whether they can help us to trace Miss Stern.
26.08.46.	David is spending a fortnights holiday with Mrs. Gensch.
02.09.46.	Informed by the Alien'ss Registration Office, 10 Piccadilly Place, W.1. that the whereabouts of Miss Stern is not known to the police.

16.12.46.	One trunk and one suitcase arrived at B.H. from Dr. Glaser's hostel Epsom. Stored in room 21??
21.05.47.	It has been decided that foster parents should be found for David who could ultimately adopt him when his mother has been presumed dead.
02.06.47.	I spoke to Mrs. Fischer and told her that she could not adopt David. I gave Miss Simmons, Birmingham, the reports received from Miss Herlitz since in her district there is a family who want an eight year old boy for adoption.
04.06.47.	I sent David Stern's particulars to Miss Simmons, B'ham hoping that the people of Coalbrrokdale, Shropshire might take him. Very good report in folder, ideal home.
28.08.47.	2 old cases open and tied and 1 old handbag transferred to?? Ref 313.
21.11.47.	David is, according to Miss Simmons report, very happy indeed.He goes to a local council school and the adoptive people have asked their own solicitor to appoint them as David's legal guardians until they can legally adopt him.
30.01.48.	David lives now at Lucklands Hotel, Mostyn Road, Colwyn Bay, North Wales. The arrangement seems to work very well.

19.04.48.	Miss Simmons rang to ask if we are a recognised adoption society. I told her that the National Adoption Society was willing to co-operate with us.
April 1949	Luggage etc belonging to Miss Stern destroyed due to bad condition.
17.11.49.	Received one Post Office book No 12813 for dispatch to Post Office Savings Bank.
18.11.49.	Returned to????
09.01.50.	David has been legally adopted on 5.1.50and his name is now David???? (a double-barrelled name)
22.09.50.	Post Office savings book sent to Miss Simmons of Birmingham Council for Refugees

I have photocopied the real case notes for your interest on the following pages.

Original case notes

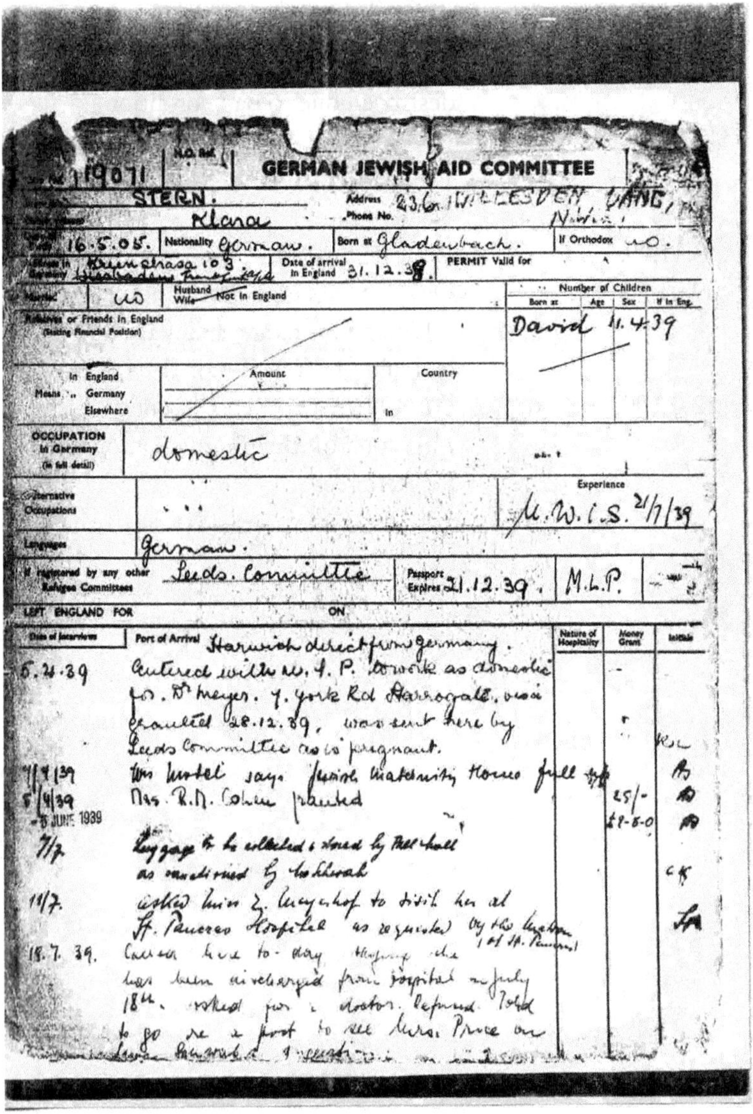

GERMAN JEWISH AID COMMITTEE

No. 19071

STERN.

Klara

Address 236 WILLESDEN LANE, N.W.

Born 16.5.05. Nationality German. Born at Gladenbach. If Orthodox no.

Address in Germany Rheinstrasse 103 Wiesbaden. Date of arrival in England 31.12.38. PERMIT Valid for

Married no. Husband/Wife Not in England

Number of Children: David 11.4.39

Relatives or Friends in England (Stating Financial Position)

Means: In England / Germany / Elsewhere — Amount — Country

OCCUPATION in Germany (in full detail): domestic

Alternative Occupations — Experience: M.W.I.S. 21/7/39

Languages: German.

If registered by any other Refugee Committees: Leeds. Committee. Passport Expires 21.12.39. M.L.P.

LEFT ENGLAND FOR ON

Port of Arrival: Harwich direct from Germany.

Date of Interview		Nature of Hospitality	Money Grant	Initials
5.4.39	Entered with M.L.P. to work as domestic for Dr Meyer. 7 York Rd Harrogate. visa granted 28.12.39. was sent here by Leeds Committee as is pregnant.			
7/4/39	Mrs Mortel says Jewish Maternity Home full up			
8/4/39	Mrs. R.N. Cohen granted		25/-	
5 JUNE 1939			£8-5-0	
7/7	Luggage to be collected & stored by Mill Hall as mentioned by Wohlfahrt			CK
11/7.	asked Miss Z. Meyerhof to visit her at St. Pancras Hospital as requested by the Lady Almoner of St. Pancras			
18.7.39.	Called here to-day saying she has been discharged from hospital on July 18th. asked for a doctor. Referred. Told to go re a post to see Mrs. Price on [illegible]			

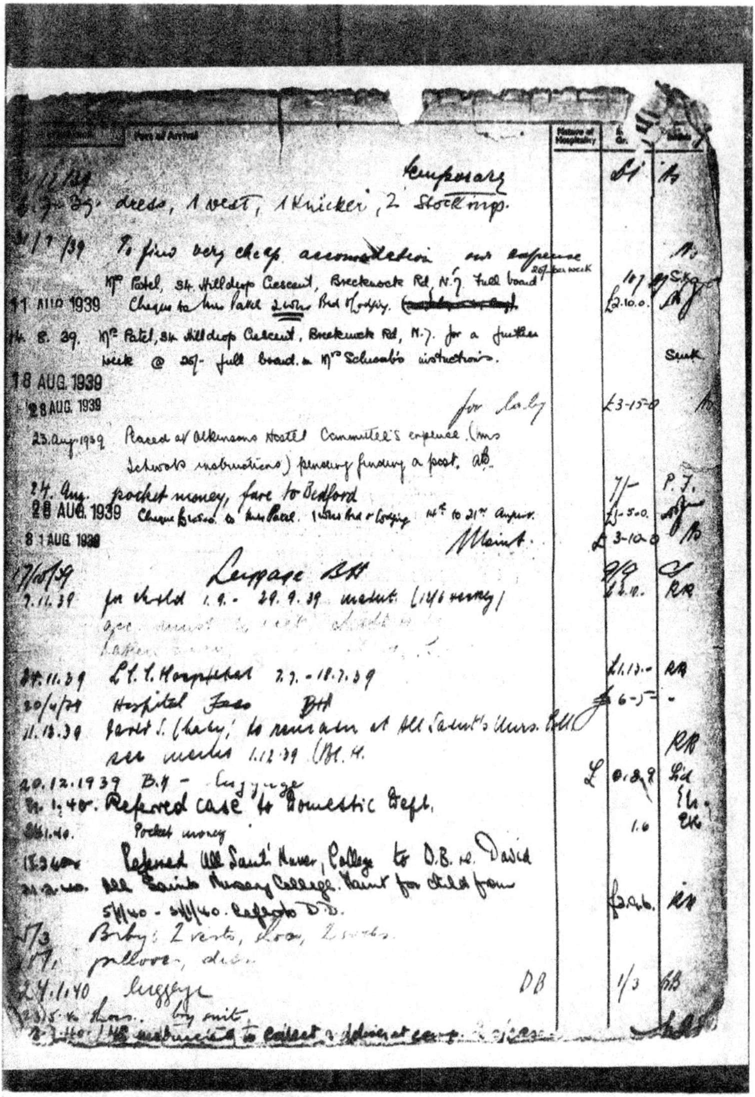

Port of Arrival | Nature of Hospitality | £ | Initials

Temporary

[illegible] 3 dress, 1 vest, 1 knicker, 2 stockings.

31/7/39 To find very cheap accommodation our expense 20/- per week

Mrs Patel, 34 Hilldrop Crescent, Brecknock Rd, N.7. Full board 10/-

11 AUG 1939 Cheque to Mrs Patel 2 weeks Bed & Lodging. £2.10.0.

14. 8. 39. Mrs Patel, 34 Hilldrop Crescent, Brecknock Rd, N.7. for a further week @ 20/- full board. on Mrs Schwab's instructions.

18 AUG 1939

28 AUG 1939 for lady £3-15-0

23.Aug.1939 Placed at Atkinsons Hostel Committee's expense (Mrs Schwab's instructions) pending finding a post.

24. Aug. pocket money, fare to Bedford 7/- P.J.

28 AUG 1939 Cheque issued to Mrs Patel 1 week bed & lodging 14th to 21st August. £1-5-0.

31 AUG 1939 Maint. £3-10-0

17/10/39 Luggage B.H. 9/9

7.11.39 for child 1.9.- 29.9.39 maint. [illegible] £2.0. RR

[illegible]

24.11.39 L.C.C. Hospital 7.7.-18.7.39 £1.13.- RR

20/4/39 Hospital Fees B.H. £6-5-

11.12.39 Janet S. (baby) to nursery at All Saint's Nurs. Coll. see minutes 1.12.39 B.H. RR

20.12.1939 B.H. - luggage £0.2.9

[illegible] 1.40. Referred case to Domestic Dept.

[illegible] 1.40. Pocket money 1.6

18.2.40 Referred All Saints' Nurs. College to D.B. re. David

21.2.40. All Saints Nursery College. Maint for child from 5/1/40 - 31/1/40. Referred to D.B. £2.2.6. RR

5/3 Baby: 2 vests, [illegible], 2 [illegible]

pullover, dress

24.1.40 luggage DB 1/3

[illegible]

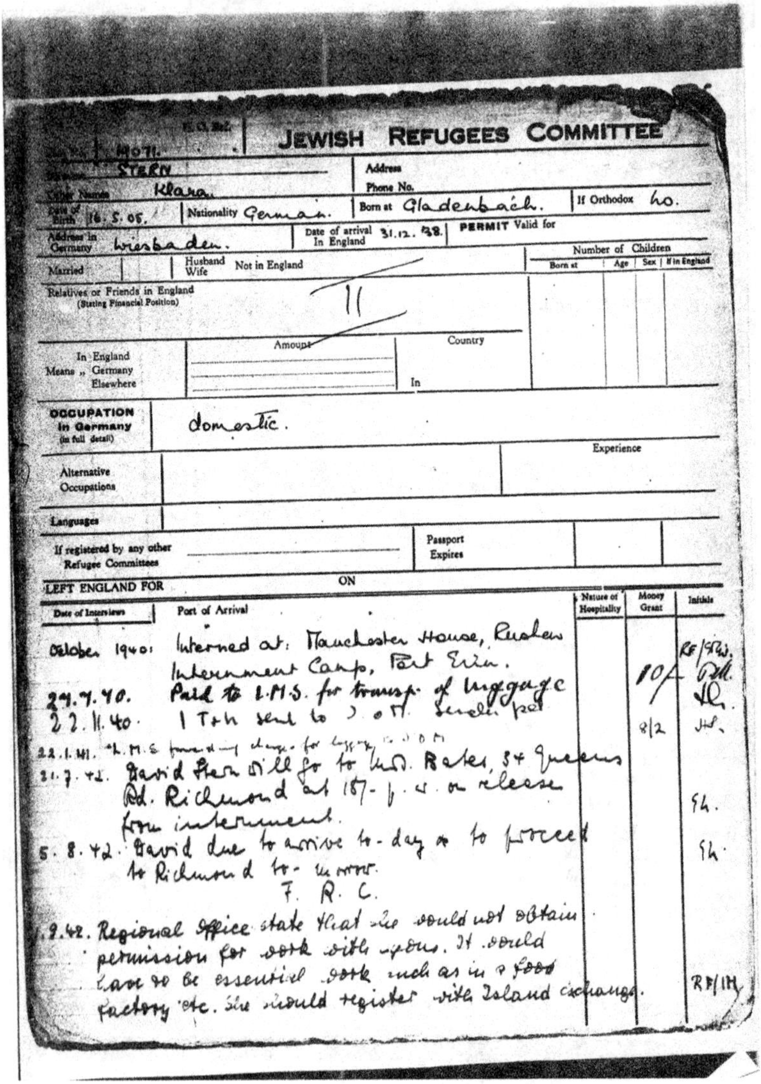

JEWISH REFUGEES COMMITTEE

H.O. Ref.

Reg. No. 14071.

Surname: STERN

Address

Phone No.

Other Names: Klara.

Date of Birth: 16. 5. 05.

Nationality: German.

Born at: Gladenbach.

If Orthodox: no.

Address in Germany: Wiesbaden.

Date of arrival In England: 31.12.38.

PERMIT Valid for

Married

Husband / Wife Not in England

Number of Children

Born at | Age | Sex | If in England

Relatives or Friends in England (Stating Financial Position)

Means In England / „ Germany / Elsewhere

Amount

Country

In

OCCUPATION in Germany (in full detail): domestic.

Alternative Occupations

Experience

Languages

If registered by any other Refugee Committees

Passport Expires

LEFT ENGLAND FOR

ON

Date of Interviews	Port of Arrival	Nature of Hospitality	Money Grant	Initials
October 1940:	Interned at: Manchester House, Rushen Internment Camp, Port Erin.			RF/SRW.
24.7.40.	Paid to L.M.S. for transp. of luggage		10/-	[illegible]
22.11.40.	1 T&h sent to I.o.M. [illegible]		8/2	[illegible]
22.1.41.	L.M.S. forwarding charges for luggage to I.O.M.			
31.7.42.	David Stern will go to Mrs. Rates, 34 Queens Rd. Richmond at 18/- p.w. on release from internment.			Sh.
5.8.42.	David due to arrive to-day & to proceed to Richmond to-morrow. F. R. C.			Sh.
.9.42.	Regional Office state that she could not obtain permission for work with you. It would have to be essential work such as in a food factory etc. She should register with Island exchange.			RF/IH.

Date of Interview	Port of Arrival	Nature of Hospitality	Money Grant	Initials
25.9.42.	David visited by Miss Smith & Mrs. Gosse – Reports in file.			G.L.
21.10.42.	Fees in future increased to 25/– p.w. Sanction given by Finance & Central Ctte.			G.L.
9.12.42.	Mother on release from Int. C. to stay for one night here at B.H. Has a job and a room to go to next day. Mr. Markey is informed.			G.S.
11.12.42.	Very good welfare report on David in file.			G.L.
7.1.43.	Arrived last night. To see A.B. re. emergency & money fares to Moulders + money for 1st week. 11, Stanley Avenue. New Malden. Surrey. To work with Messrs. Senior + Co Ltd. Raynes Park. S.W.20. as a factory hand.			G.S.
7.1.43.	Mrs. Stern will go to see David to-morrow afternoon.			G.L.
7.1.1943.	Signed A.B. form (Provincial Case). – Copy in file.			F.G.
25.1.43	Has started work, wages £2.15.0. p.w. Asks for clothing grant.			G.F.
1.2.43	I saw woman when she called at B.H. on Saturday morning (30.1.43) [illegible] an interview [illegible] Miss Fellner as she is dealing with case.			R.G.
2.2.43.	Calling here having a cut in her hand. (Outpatient of Nelson Hospital) We phoned Med. Supr. who informed us that she was unfit for work for a short time only having had 3 stitches in her right hand. She has to see them again on Thursday. We persuade her to return to her lodging and not to move. Transfer to Miss Fellner.			G.S.
2/2/43.	This very excitable lady after her long internment appears to have no clothes left. We have no luggage of her – [illegible]			

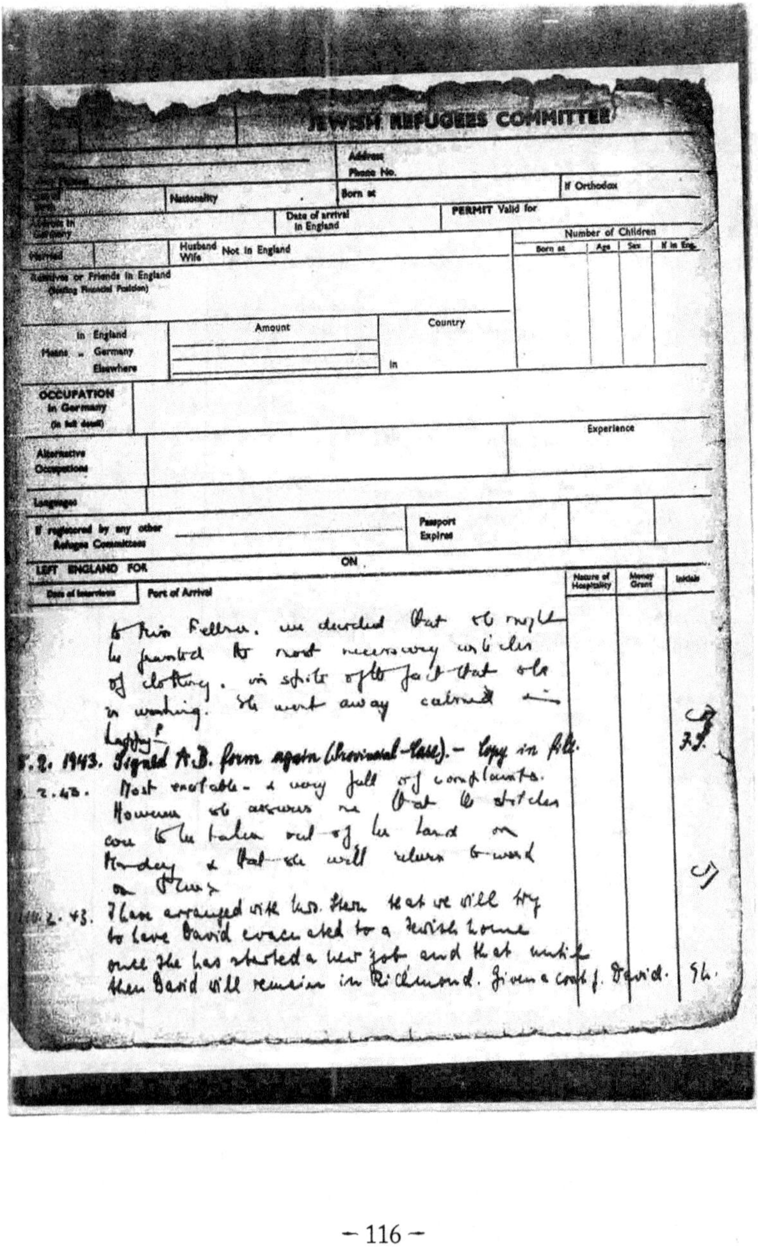

JEWISH REFUGEES COMMITTEE

Address
Phone No.

Nationality | Born at | If Orthodox

Address in Germany | Date of arrival in England | PERMIT Valid for

Married | Husband / Wife Not in England | Number of Children: Born at | Age | Sex | If in Eng.

Relatives or Friends in England (Stating Financial Position)

Means in England / Germany / Elsewhere | Amount | Country | in

OCCUPATION in Germany (in full detail) | Experience

Alternative Occupations

Languages

If registered by any other Refugee Committees | Passport Expires

LEFT ENGLAND FOR | ON

Date of Interview | Port of Arrival | Nature of Hospitality | Money Grant | Initials

to Miss Fellner. we decided that she might be granted the most necessary articles of clothing. in spite of the fact that she is working. She went away calmed & happy! — [illegible]

5.2.1943. Signed A.B. form again (Provisional-Case). — Copy in file. — F.F.

[illegible] 2.43. Most excitable — & very full of complaints. However she assures me that the stitches are to be taken out of her hand on Monday & that she will return to work on [illegible] — [illegible]

[illegible] 2.43. I have arranged with Mrs. Stern that we will try to have David evacuated to a Jewish home once she has started a new job and that until then David will remain in Richmond. Given a coat f. David. — Sh.

Part of Arrival	Nature of Hospitality	Money Grant	Initials

[illegible].2.43. At the request of Miss Fellner we take her to our Homefield Hostel, 14 Belsize Sq. N.W.3 as from to-morrow (on 1.2.43) until fit for work again after an accident. Claimed Workman's Compensation. Has about £1. 30/- savings. [illegible] B 9 [illegible] Will refund her Workman's Compensation. — Housing A.T.

[illegible].2.43. Hospital says: "fit for work as from 18.2.43." Will work in a different Department of same Factory. (Senior & Co Ltd. Raynes Park. S.W.20) Manager will send her an address to here in time. Wimbledon – Kingston L.E. did not grant her release but thinks that a transfer to another Dep. will make work easier for her. — J.S.

She will return to Moulden 17.2.43. — J.S.

15.2.43. Miss Wheeler (Hanover House) phones manager of Messrs. Senior & Co. They haven't got the release form. He [illegible] a room for her and wants to see her this afternoon. Miss [illegible] will start with [illegible] again

17.2.43 Will leave Homefield to day, to 307 Kingston Rd. S.W.20. Will start work again to-morrow. Received up to now one week's compensation of 27/-, but has to pay rent [illegible] and other expenses until she receives her first salary. She promised to pay the [illegible] for [illegible] days' maintenance in Homefield Hostel à 3/6 per day in instalments during the next weeks. — Housing A.T.

22.2.43 Left Homefield on 17.2.43. — Housing

9.4.1943. Signed A.B. form again (Provincial Case). – Copy in file. — J.S.

16.4.43. Med. cert. recv. Unfit for work for 14 days. — [illegible]

16 JUNE 1943 Repayment re Homefield Hostel – £1.1.0 — [illegible]

23.8.43. [illegible] from Mrs. [illegible] received from [illegible], sent to Mr. Samson for [illegible]

25.8.43. She stayed with Miss [illegible] 1st – 4th August 43. and missed £4 out of her handbag which she left in her room whilst she went downstairs for dinner. The local Police (Sergeant Taylor) have taken the case up and made all enquiries on the spot. — [illegible]

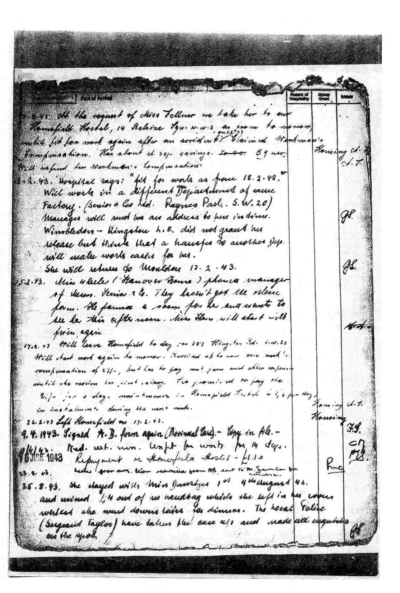

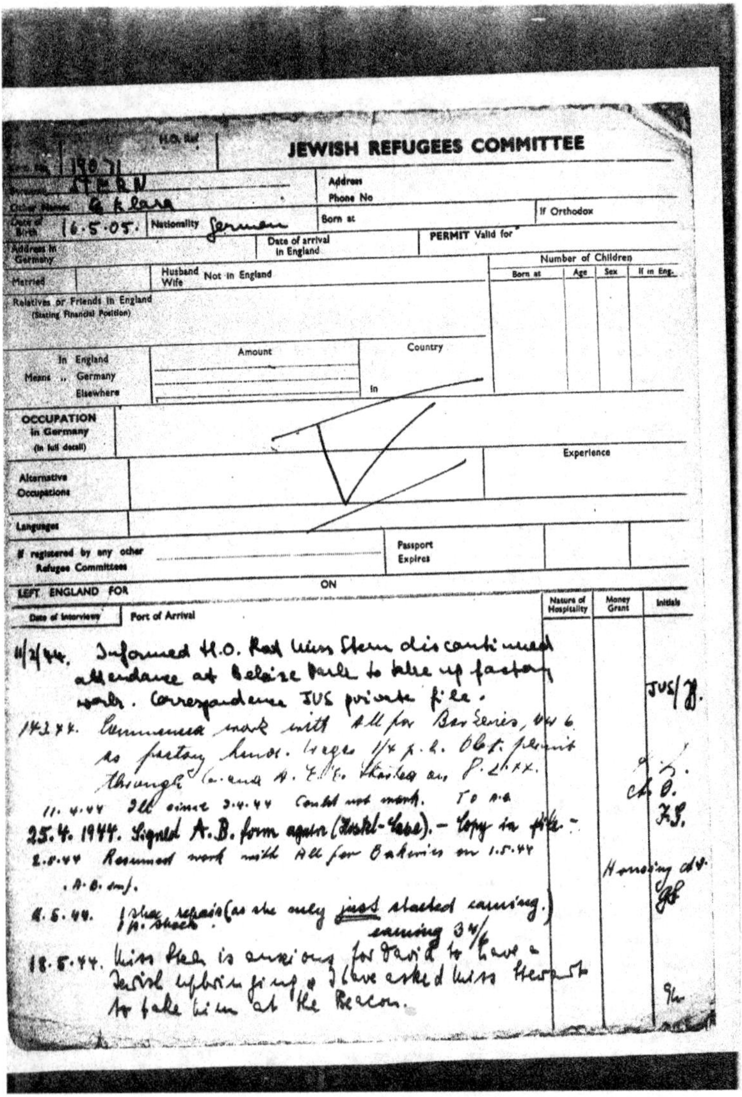

JEWISH REFUGEES COMMITTEE

Card No. 19871 · H.O. Ref.
Surname: STERN
Other Names: G. Klara
Date of Birth: 16.5.05. · Nationality: German
Address in Germany
Address · Phone No
Born at · If Orthodox
Date of arrival in England · PERMIT Valid for
Married · Husband / Wife: Not in England
Number of Children: Born at · Age · Sex · If in Eng.
Relatives or Friends in England (Stating Financial Position)
Means: In England / Germany / Elsewhere · Amount · Country · in
OCCUPATION in Germany (in full detail)
Alternative Occupations · Experience
Languages
If registered by any other Refugee Committees · Passport Expires
LEFT ENGLAND FOR · ON
Date of Interview · Port of Arrival · Nature of Hospitality · Money Grant · Initials

11/2/44. Informed H.O. that Miss Stern discontinued attendance at Belsize Park to take up factory work. Correspondence JUS private file. — JUS/[illegible]
14.3.44. Commenced work with All for Bar Series, W6 as factory hand. Wages [illegible] p.h. Obt. permit through [illegible] and A. E. E. [illegible] on 8.2.44. — [illegible]
11.4.44 Ill since 3.4.44 Could not work. To A.B. — [illegible]
25.4.1944. Signed A.B. form again (Hostel-Case). – Copy in file. — F.S.
2.5.44 Resumed work with All for Bakeries on 1.5.44. A.B. emp. — Housing dt.
4.5.44. [illegible] repairs (as she only just started earning.) earning 34/- — [illegible]
18.5.44. Miss Stern is anxious for David to have a Jewish upbringing & I have asked Miss [illegible] to take him at the Beacon. — [illegible]

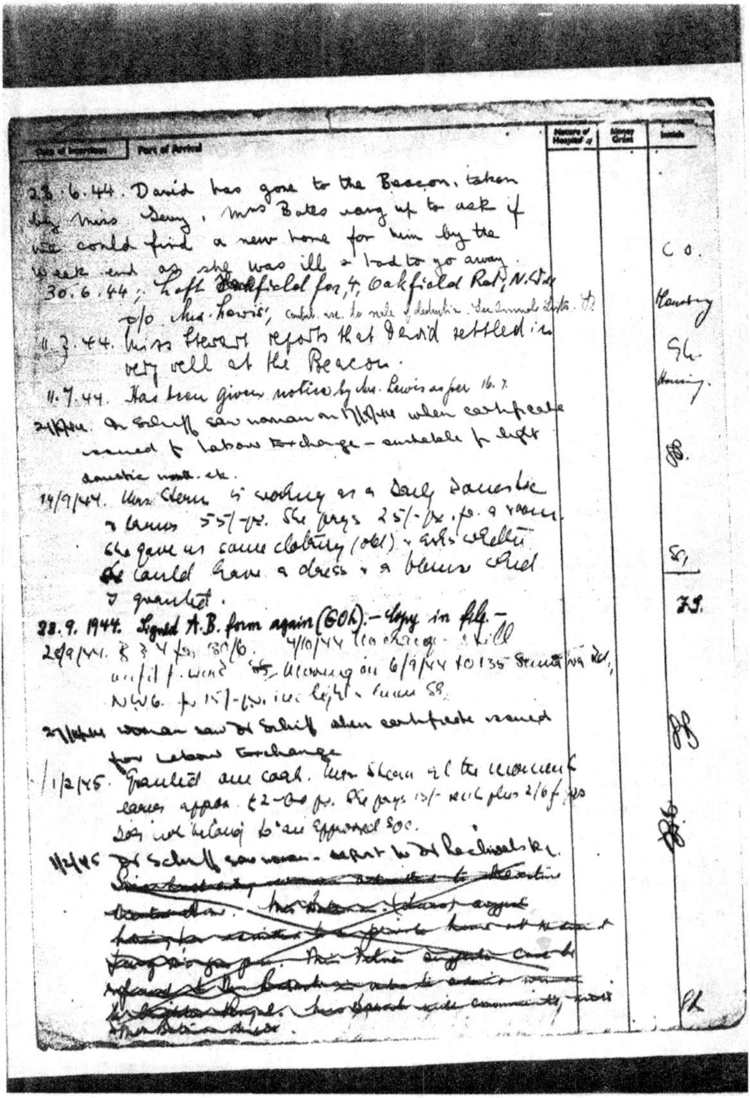

Date of Interview | Port of Arrival

Nature of Help | Money Grant | Initials

23.6.44. David has gone to the Beacon, taken by Miss Seny. Mrs Bates rang up to ask if we could find a new home for him by the week end as she was ill & had to go away. — C.O.

30.6.44; Left Oakfield for, 4, Oakfield Rd, N.[illegible] c/o Mrs. Lewis; [illegible] — Hawtrey

11.7.44. Miss Stewart reports that David settled in very well at the Beacon. — [illegible]

11.7.44. Has been given notice by Mrs. Lewis as per 16.7. — Hawtrey.

24/[illegible]. Dr Schiff saw woman on [illegible] when certificate issued for Labour Exchange – suitable for light domestic work etc. — [illegible]

14/9/44. Mrs Stern is working as a daily domestic & earns 55/- p.w. She pays 25/- p.w. for a room. She gave us some clothing (old) & [illegible] She could have a dress & a blouse [illegible] I granted. — [illegible]

28.9.1944. Signed A.B. form again (GOh). – Copy in file. — F.S.

2[illegible]/9/44. [illegible] 4/10/44 [illegible] still unfit for work [illegible] moving on 6/9/44 to 135 [illegible] Rd, N.W.6. [illegible] 15/- [illegible] light & [illegible]

27/[illegible] woman saw Dr Schiff when certificate issued for Labour Exchange — [illegible]

1/2/45. Granted [illegible] cash. Mrs Stern is at the moment earning approx £2-0-0 p.w. She pays 15/- rent plus 2/6 for [illegible] Does not belong to an approved Soc. — [illegible]

1/2/45 Dr Schiff saw woman – report to Dr Rachwalski.

~~[illegible]~~ — [illegible]

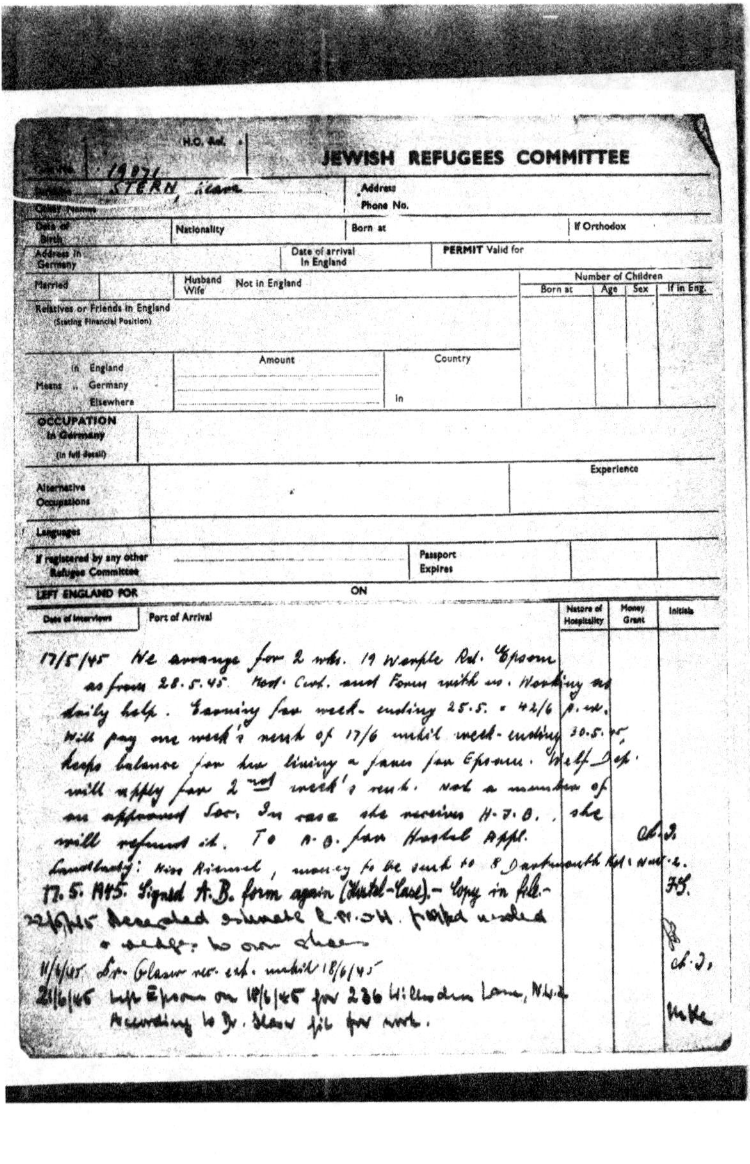

H.O. Ref.

Case No. 19871

JEWISH REFUGEES COMMITTEE

Surname STERN, Klara

Other Names

Address

Phone No.

Date of Birth | Nationality | Born at | If Orthodox

Address in Germany | Date of arrival in England | PERMIT Valid for

Married | Husband / Wife | Not in England

Number of Children: Born at | Age | Sex | If in Eng.

Relatives or Friends in England (Stating Financial Position)

Means in England / " Germany / Elsewhere | Amount | Country | In

OCCUPATION in Germany (in full detail)

Alternative Occupations | Experience

Languages

If registered by any other Refugee Committee | Passport Expires

LEFT ENGLAND FOR | ON

Date of Interviews	Port of Arrival	Nature of Hospitality	Money Grant	Initials
17/5/45	We arrange for 2 wks. 19 Worple Rd. Epsom as from 28.5.45. Med. Cert. and Form with us. Working as daily help. Earning for week-ending 25.5. = 42/6 p.w. Will pay one week's rent of 17/6 until week-ending 30.5.45, keeps balance for her living & fares for Epsom. Welf. Dep. will apply for 2nd week's rent. Not a member of an approved Soc. In case she receives H.T.B., she will refund it. To A.B. for Hostel Appl.			[illegible]
	Landlady: Miss Riemel, money to be sent to 8 Dartmouth Rd. NW.2.			
17.5.1945.	Signed A.B. form again (Hostel-Case). – Copy in file. –			F.S.
22/5/45	[illegible]			[illegible]
11/6/45	Dr. Glaser rec. ext. until 18/6/45			[illegible]
21/6/45	Left Epsom on 18/6/45 for 236 Willesden Lane, NW.2. According to Dr. Glaser fit for work.			[illegible]

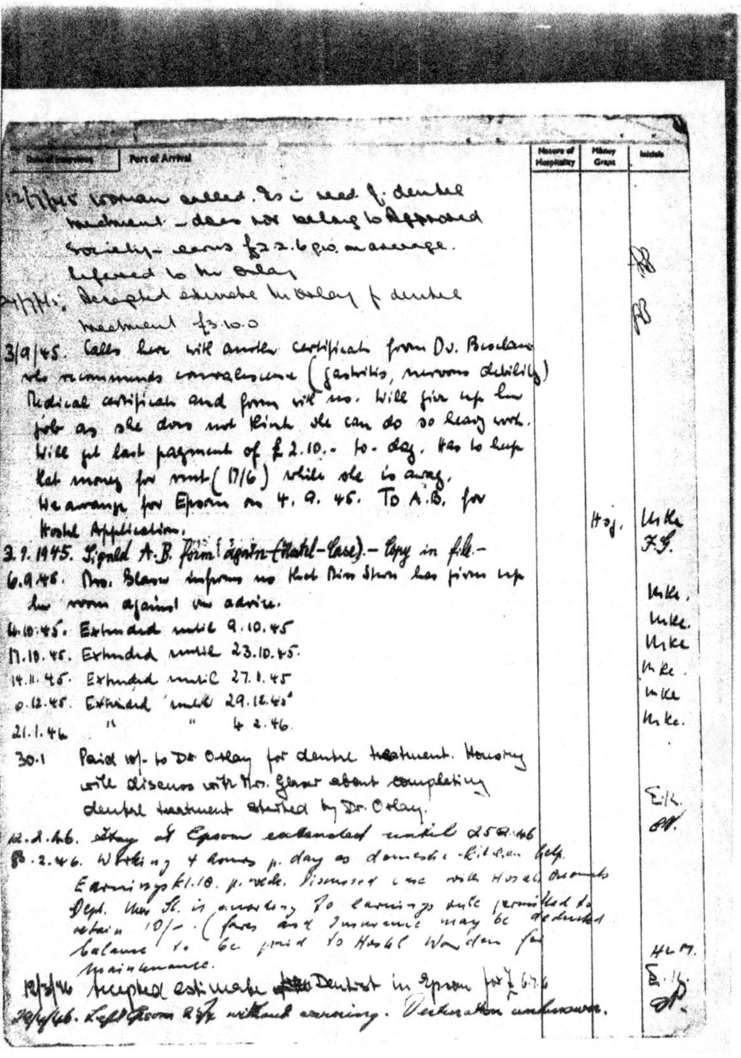

Detail Interviews / Port of Arrival	Nature of Hospitality	Money Grant	Initials
12/7/45 Woman called. Is in need of dental treatment — does not belong to Approved Society — earns £2.2.6 p.w. on average. Referred to Dr Oslay			AB
24/7/45: Accepted estimate Dr Oslay for dental treatment £3.10.0			AB
3/9/45. Calls here with another certificate from Dr. Brodan who recommends convalescence (gastritis, nervous debility). Medical certificate and form with us. Will give up her job as she does not think she can do so heavy work. Will get last payment of £2.10.- to-day. Has to keep that money for rent (17/6) while she is away. We arrange for Epsom on 4.9.45. To A.B. for Hostel Application.		Hosp.	Mike
3.9.1945. Signed A.B. form! again (Hotel-Case). — Copy in file.—			F.G.
6.9.45. Mrs. Glaser informs us that Miss Stein has given up her room against our advice.			Mike.
4.10.45. Extended until 9.10.45			Mike.
17.10.45. Extended until 23.10.45.			Mike
14.11.45. Extended until 27.1.45			Mike.
6.12.45. Extended until 29.12.45			Mike
21.1.46 " " 4.2.46.			Mike.
30.1 Paid 10/- to Dr Oslay for dental treatment. Housing will discuss with Mrs. Glaser about completing dental treatment started by Dr. Oslay.			E.K.
12.2.46. Stay at Epsom extended until 25.2.46			AV.
18.2.46. Working 4 hours p. day as domestic kitchen help. Earnings £1.10. p. week. Discussed case with Hostel Accounts Dept. Miss St. is according to earnings rule permitted to retain 10/-. (fares and Insurance may be deducted) balance to be paid to Hostel Warden for maintenance.			H.M.
12/3/46 Accepted estimate of Dentist in Epsom for £6.7.6			E.K.
16/4/46. Left Epsom 2/4 without warning. Destination unknown.			AP.

JEWISH REFUGEES COMMITTEE

H.O. Ref.

Case No. 1907.

Surname STERN,

Other Names Klara,

Address

Phone No.

Date of Birth

Nationality

Born at

If Orthodox

Address in Germany

Date of arrival in England

PERMIT Valid for

Married

Husband / Wife Not in England

Number of Children

Born at	Age	Sex	If in Eng.

Relatives or Friends in England (Stating Financial Position)

Means		Amount	Country
in	England		
,,	Germany		
	Elsewhere		In

OCCUPATION in Germany (in full detail)

Experience

Alternative Occupations

Languages

If registered by any other Refugee Committee

Passport Expires

LEFT ENGLAND FOR ON

Date of Interviews	Port of Arrival	Nature of Hospitality	Money Grant	Initials
21.8.1946.	Writing to the Special Investigations Branch, New Scotland Yard asking whether they can help us to trace Mrs. Stern.			BM/S.
26. 8. 46.	David is [illegible] [illegible] [illegible] [illegible] with [illegible] [illegible].			[illegible]
2.9.1946.	Informed by the Aliens registration Office, 10, Piccadilly Place, W1 that the present whereabouts of the [illegible] [illegible] known to the Police			BM/S.
16. 12. 46	The trunk & one s/case arrived at B.H. [illegible] [illegible]'s Hostel, [illegible]. Stored in [illegible]			[illegible]
21. 5. 47.	It has now been decided that a foster [illegible] should be found for David [illegible] could [illegible] adopt him when his mother can be [illegible] dead. [illegible]			
2. 6. 47.	I spoke to Mrs. Fischer [illegible] told her that she could not adopt David. I gave Miss Simmons B'ham the report received from Miss [illegible] since in [illegible]			

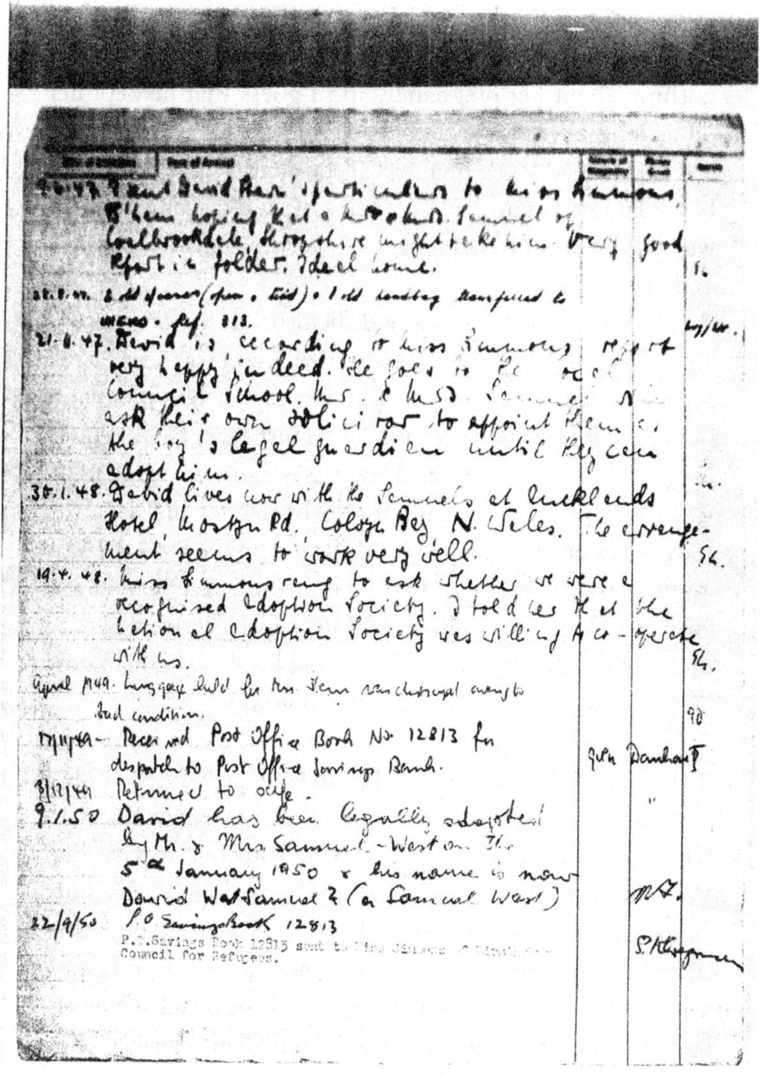

26.4.47. I sent David Kern's [?] particulars to Miss Simmons B'ham hoping that a Mr & Mrs. Samuel of Coalbrookdale Shropshire might take him. Very good report in folder. Ideal home.

25.8.47. 2 old jerseys ([illegible]) & 1 old handbag transferred to WEMO. Ref. 813.

21.8.47. David is according to Miss Simmons' report very happy indeed. He goes to the local Council School. Mr. & Mrs. Samuel [illegible] ask their own solicitor to appoint them as the boy's legal guardian until they can adopt him.

30.1.48. David lives now with the Samuels at [illegible] Hotel, Mostyn Rd. Colwyn Bay N. Wales. The arrangement seems to work very well.

19.4.48. Miss Simmons rang to ask whether we were a recognised Adoption Society. I told her that the National Adoption Society was willing to co-operate with us.

April 1949. Luggage held for Mr. Kern [illegible] bad condition.

17/11/49 – Received Post Office Book No 12813 for despatch to Post Office Savings Bank.

3/12/49 Returned to safe.

9.1.50 David has been legally adopted by Mr. & Mrs. Samuel-West on the 5th January 1950 & his name is now David West-Samuel ? (or Samuel West)

22/9/50 P.O. Savings Book 12813

P.O.Savings Book 12813 sent to Miss Simmons [illegible] Council for Refugees.

The information on what was happening to Klara at the time is taken from her factual case notes, and later on from information from the archivist in the Isle of Man. You will see that when she went to Dr. Meyer in Harrogate, he knew nothing about her pregnancy, and I guess that he kept her on as long as it was socially decent to do so. She returned to London and saw a member of the charity that dealt with her. Klara had many bed-sit addresses, and it seems that she was in and out of hospitals, both before David was born, and after.

The case notes are really difficult to decipher; there is an entry on 5.4.1939 which states that Klara was sent by the 'Leeds Committee' back to London as she was pregnant, her due date being 10th April. She must have been heavily pregnant by this date, as David was born on 11.4.1939. On 7.4.1939 an entry said that 'Mrs Motel has said the Jewish Maternity Hospital was full' and on the 8th Klara was granted money. Was that to pay for medical care? David was born at 24 Underwood Road, Whitechapel - we were later to find that this was a Jewish Maternity Hospital. I don't know if it was the same one Mrs Motel referred to.

There is a gap then of the entries in the case notes of 3 months, and the next entry refers to luggage being collected and stored, costing money. The following entry refers to Klara being in hospital and wanting someone to visit her. Was she suffering from post-natal depression? Did it start as soon as David was born or later? The records show that soon after David was born in London, he was taken to a residential nursery in Harrogate. He was subsequently reunited with his mother in 1940, and then together, they were interned on the Isle of Man, after being subjected to pressure from the welfare workers for Klara to give David up for adoption.

In response to the radio broadcast in September 1939, 'Britain is at war with Germany', the British Public classed other people as 'friendly' or 'alien'. Klara came into the 'alien' category. Fear of 'the Jews' was as pronounced in England as in Germany. Jews in England had to report their movements to the police. They were forbidden to own a map of any kind, a camera, a radio, a bicycle or a car. The sheer ignorance of most British people about the situation in Germany meant that Klara was given very little sympathy.

In September 1939, just after *the* radio broadcast, tribunals were set up to classify every alien in the country. All aliens were kept in special centres until classification, and they could not go to the toilet without being watched. Those eventually classed as category A were very dangerous people indeed, and immediately went to prison. Category B were judged as a suspicious alien, and only category C were just about OK to live with others. B category aliens were not allowed to change their place of residence without informing the police, and they were given a special 'aliens registration book,' which contained their left thumb print. Klara was classed as category C, and she must have thought 'out of the frying pan, into the fire!'

From December 1939 to May 1940, press articles whipped up paranoia amongst the British people. On the 12th May 1940, the Home Office ordered that all German and Austrian males over 16 and under 60 must be interned, regardless of category.

On 14th May 1940, Neville Bland (Minister at The Hague) said, "The paltriest kitchen maid, with German connections, not only can be but generally is a menace to the safety of the country. I have not the least doubt that when the signal is given – there will be satellites of the monster all over the country who will at once embark on widespread sabotage and attacks on civilians and the military indiscriminately. We cannot afford to take the risk. All must be interned." (Isle of Man Examiner June 7th 1943)

All aliens had to appear before a tribunal, where they were asked the question "Have you got any relatives in Germany?" 'Yes' brought a grade B. Many of the people sitting on tribunal panels were anti-German and anti-semite.

Every day there were reports of battles between the British and Germans, and Scotland Yard raised their concerns about the number of aliens in Britain. Articles in the newspapers demanded 'intern the lot now!' Already the category A aliens were imprisoned, the women being sent to Holloway Jail, and an article on May 13th 1940 said, "There will be no security - only when all of them are safely under guard. We must see them all behind barbed wire."

The Government's response to this was, "There is a Government plan to take into custody and intern all aliens – including women." Just after this, the Isle of Man Examiner (June 7th 1940) fired by news from the mainland said, "There is only one place for the enemy alien whilst the war lasts. That place is behind barbed wire on this Island just like in WW1." This opinion was expressed with the strongest possible emphasis by the House of Keys, the Manx Government. It was decided that enemy aliens fell into 3 categories.

Grade A – These were Nazi sympathisers and were sent immediately to Holloway prison.
Grade B – These women were seen as a threat and were to have restricted freedom.
Grade C – Refugees from Nazi control.

On 27th May 1940 about 3,000 women resident in Great Britain and of German origin were under suspicion; they were often separated from their husbands and children, but this didn't happen to Klara (now 36) in that she had no husband. She was woken up very early one morning by the police hammering on her door in the place where she was living, and told to bring only what she could carry. At this time, the same was happening all over the British Isles. Hundreds of officials waiting in Black Marias spread through London in preparation for the mass arrests. At 8.0am they were knocking on all doors. On 27th May 1940, Chief Constables all over the country received orders to arrest B category women. The instruction was to arrest women early in the morning, and police searched their houses. Mothers with children under 6 could take their children with them. They were told to wear and pack warm clothing, and to bring a blanket. By noon that day, 3,500 women had been arrested nationwide. This included 1,500 women in London (mostly domestic servants, as this was the only way to get a visa.)

Klara was told to hurry up, and informed of what she could take with her. This was a small suitcase, one blanket, and David. She was told to expect to be away for two or three days; in fact she was interned a long time (one of the longest: until January 1943). Klara was forced to hand over her ration book; she was not told what was happening nor where she was going, and must have been very frightened. She was then taken to Fulham gymnasium, and after much questioning, she stayed the night there, sleeping on the floor. Klara and the other women were watched constantly, and were not allowed to shut the door when they went to the toilet.

Only A grade were sent to prison (200 women) and B grade were interned on the Isle of Man. All domestic servants, the unemployed, and those in refugee hostels were graded B. Husbands and wives were put into different categories, in that one could be A or B and one could be C. Category B women were the first to be interned on the Isle of Man, and Klara was among the first arrivals on the Island on May 30th 1940. In the early days of the internment, there was no attempt at separation. All the women were rushed to the Island, and Jews, Nazis and Fascists were all placed living together, sometimes even sharing the same bed. There were 18 B detainees who were considered dangerous. Then after a while, the women were separated into different hotels.

To give a flavour, there is a quote from a woman who carried out the arrests. "We are requested to arrest her immediately and stay with her until she is brought to the retention centre. She can take what she can carry with one arm. She can also bring a mat or blanket to sleep on." On arrest, one woman said, "I have done nothing." "You have done plenty and are in worse trouble than you know," was the reply. All the women carried gas masks, and there were among them nuns, mothers, babies, children and older women. Some of the women were fashionably dressed, and some were self-confessed high class prostitutes.

Klara was taken to Liverpool, along with many other German Jewish women, on a crowded train, standing all the way. She was made to walk in double file through the streets of Liverpool, herded like cattle to the train to take them to the port. Liverpool housewives and many others jeered at the 'Nazis,' shouting insults such as "filthy Krauts" as they boarded the 'Ben-my-Cree' ferry to sail to the Isle of Man. I suppose this was a change from 'filthy Jews!' This must have echoed Nazi Germany for Klara – long lines of women and children, clutching a few belongings and walking up a long, long road. The best is though, at least she was going to live. Klara arrived, after a very rough crossing in October 1940, when she was sick once again.

The case notes say – 'Interned at Manchester house, Rushaw Internment Camp, Port Erin, Isle of Man.' But they do not give any flavour of the journey Klara made, or what she was witness to on the way.

On arrival, they were marched from the boat to the train. The Isle of Man local people watched and spat on them. There were long lines of women and children, clutching a few belongings, and they were herded up the long road. Key words here are – separation, bewilderment, resilience, hope and faith.

Photo of Klara taken by MI5

FEMALE." 7160

REGISTRATION CARD.

(1) NAME (Surname first in Roman capitals). STERN Klara

ALIAS

(2) IDENTITY BOOK OR REGISTRATION CERTIFICATE.
No. 689651
Date 4. 1. 39.
Issued at Harrogate.

(3) NATIONALITY German Born on 16. 5. 05 in Gladenbach

(4) PREVIOUS NATIONALITY (if any)

(5) PROFESSION or OCCUPATION Domestic

(6) Arrived in U.K. on 31/12/38
" " Isle of Man 30/5/40.

(7) Address of last residence outside U.K. Frankfurt a/M.

SINGLE or MARRIED married.

Husband's Name and Serial No.

(8) GOVERNMENT SERVICE

(9) PASSPORT or other papers as to nationality and identity.
German pass 1241/38.
Wiesbaden
22. 12. 38.

(11) SIGNATURE OR LEFT THUMB PRINT.

DPBU 209/a

When Klara herself arrived at the dock in the Isle of Man, she had to walk to the train station and catch on old

Victorian train from Douglas to Port Erin. On the train, the women were singing to try to keep their spirits up. Klara surely must have wondered what was happening, tired and alone except for a seventeen month old child, and carrying a heavy case and blanket. On reaching Port Erin she had to walk from the train station to gather at St. Catherine's church. She was then given a piece of paper with an address on it and told to make her own way there. She joined groups of women who were wandering around, not knowing where to go. Klara finally discovered that Manchester House was high on the hill to the right of Port Erin, and started to walk. She was really tired by the time she got there, as it was a long way from the church and all uphill, and so was David with his little legs.

Map of Port Erin

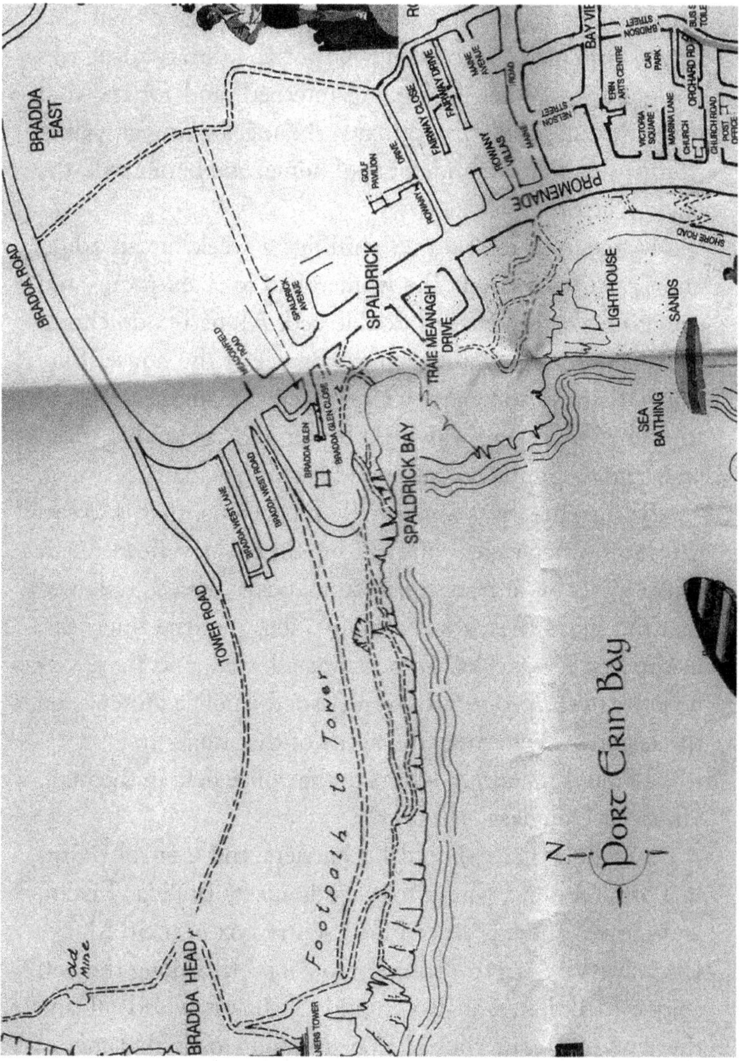

Manchester House was a boarding house, and she was given a room to share with another woman. She too was German but a Nazi sympathiser, so it was not an ideal situation for Klara. But she decided that other than this fact, (she hoped it would not be for the duration), it was not going to be too bad being interned, and for the first time since she had left Germany, she was looking at rolling countryside that reminded her of home, and better still, the sea was just there.

Hoteliers were paid 28 shillings a week for an adult, and 12/6d for a child. The women had to share rooms and sometimes had to share a double bed. All had to do chores in the house. Depending on the owner of the house, food was not always adequate. Kippers were a main meal a lot of the time, and there was little butter and eggs. This, from an island community that prided itself on its dairy farming.

Rushen area was abnormally prosperous, that is to say, the shops which were profiting from the business from aliens. There was a lot of resentment from locals, who complained that the shops were always full of aliens. For the Internees, in the first few weeks, no post was allowed, and there was no news of the progress of war. Also, the police presence on the Island grew to meet the needs of the situation.

Taken from admin letters to the police held in the main library at Douglas:

30.5.40 'There should be barriers and control points in Port Erin and where four roads meet, Bradda, Fistard and Howe. There is a need for a sentry box near St. Mary's Church. Wire ran from the sea to Zion Hill, along the golf course to Ballafesson Rd, Bradda Hill was wired off and there was 24 hour control from the four roads that met at Port St Mary.'

The object of the control was to prevent the aliens from leaving the area, unless they have a permit. There was to be a constable on duty who would stop all vehicles and persons. Passes would only be granted in exceptional circumstances, and these were to be scrutinised carefully. British subjects were not allowed onto the island without an ID card. Business must be of a tangible nature, and there was to be a stop and search for any 'carry out' letters from aliens.

Dame Joanna Cruikshank was appointed as Camp Commandant. She had been a nursing sister and previously matron in charge of the British Red Cross in England. She was a harsh disciplinarian who applied the rules rigorously, and many women wrote letters of complaint to the Home Office. (I read some of her letters when I was researching and they were rude and racist). Joanna Cruikshank found out about the letters, and summoned the women, accusing them of betrayal. It was the practice to issue permits to local residents for them to go to the foreshore, on condition that they did not enter into conversation with aliens. If they did so, they were liable to prosecution. In the very hot summer of 1940 Cruikshank complained that women were swimming in their underwear, and called them "Immoral Europeans'. Then in October 1940, there was a request from her, asking for daylight control in order to stop aliens getting out to the breakwater. In a letter dated 26.10.40 she wrote, "We need men of the right type to control the area. If you only knew the perversity of these people and their desire to roam!" She believed that the women went after any male they could find, and that no man was safe. "Women will even go out with men on the fishing boats," she said. Joanna Cruikshank was constantly arguing and at loggerheads with the local police and the Home Office.

Local women in particular wanted to enter Port Erin freely, and the contents of a letter to the police from Joanna Cruikshank in relation to this, read:

"I would add that I fail to see the argument that the residents in the Bradda district are suffering great hardship as a result of this control. I realise how infinitesimal this inconvenience may be, compared to what fellow countrymen elsewhere have to put up with but …"

She finally left in May 1941, and was replaced by a Mr. Cuthbert, a man who seemed more amenable.

Policewomen were volunteering to work on the Isle of Man, and they were all taken from London forces. All of them were between twenty to thirty years of age. They started to arrive on 24.7.40, escorting Category B alien women who had previously been held as prisoners in Holloway HMP. The fare from London per head was 14s 6d.

The following information was found in the police records at the library in the Isle of Man:

Some of the police women were: Sgt. Flo Pike – origin Wiltshire, Con Elizabeth Hind – Scotland, Con Ivy Baxter – London, Con Emily Layram – Northants, Con Ellen Pole – London, Con Joyce Ball – London. She was called back home to Dulwich 21.10.40 as her family home had been bombed due to enemy action. There is also a specific mention of a police woman, Rose Nial, who arrived in November 1940, recorded as being on relief duty.

It seems that there was nothing that these policewomen would not do for the German women, and a culture developed where they became known as 'helpful' to the aliens.

Life as an internee was not all bad. Klara made great friends, and it was soon after her arrival at Manchester House that things there improved, in that she no longer had to share a room. But depression continued to spread amongst the internees, which led to desperation. They began to grow their own vegetables, and they were also encouraged to knit, and make articles from parachute silk. These articles were then sold in London.

Christmas 1940 saw a lot of entertainment over that period, and the film 'Pinnochio' was shown. By July 1941, all aliens were allowed to shop on Mondays and Wednesdays during the afternoon, and to use the beach, where there was a separated area on the beach for them. On all other days, locals shopped and used the beach, and the internees were still seen as an unwelcome nuisance by the locals. By April 1942, tourists and visitors were back on the Island for holidays, which included Port Erin. This was encouraged by the Manx Government, in order to make up for lost revenue. Also, there was a decrease in the number of internees, as many of them had been released after one year. All of those who remained were congregated into the Bradda area, (which was the area where Klara lived.)

On release, women were offered the choice of going to London or joining the ATS. By August 1942, only 3,400 internees were left on the island; this figure included all the men on the other side of the island.

On reading documents in Douglas library, I found the following memories of a seven year old girl.

Ellen's Story (found in the archives in the library -Imprisoned with her family as enemy aliens.)

My parents and I had moved to Britain in 1936 to get away from the problems Jewish families were having, but after the outbreak of the war, my father had no papers to say that he was a 'friendly' alien. We were taken to the Isle of Man to be interned there in a camp for enemy aliens. I was only seven years old at the time, and it was all very hard to understand. I remember my father being taken away to the men's internment centre Onchan in Douglas. I didn't know where or why he had gone or why my mother was crying. A week later we were also taken to a reception centre in Liverpool before being taken to Port Erin as it now is, where the women were kept. I vividly remember hundreds of us being made to walk in a long crocodile down to the docks. The roads were closed to let us through, and the streets were lined with soldiers armed with open bayonets – being seven years old, they were right at my eye level. I didn't know why they were pointed at us. Behind the soldiers, the people from Liverpool crowded the pavements and actually jeered us, hurling insults. It was very confusing. We took a ferry overnight to get to the island. I remember having to sleep on the steps of the ship, it was so crowded. At Port Erin the women were boarded with local guesthouses, who were glad of the opportunity to make some extra money. I became friends with Eileen, the daughter of the woman who ran our boarding house. We didn't receive any schooling, so I used to accompany her to school as far as the tall, barbed wire fences where she was allowed to continue and I was met with open bayonets again. They are the strongest image I retain, simply because I couldn't understand why they were pointed at me. Every day the women were bussed to a local football pitch where they did agricultural work, turning the pitch into a place to grow turnips. The only food I remember from this time, although we must have received more, was toast done over an open fire and raw turnips. Although we were not kept with my father, once a month the women and children at Port Erin were bussed over to Onchan to visit their men-folk, which I remember as being a journey full of tears. I was there for 16 months, during which time I developed a very severe inferiority complex from so obviously being viewed as a second class citizen – by the jeering Liverpuddlians as we marched to the ferry, by the tyrannical female Commandant, and by the soldiers with their open bayonets who wouldn't let me through the gates where my friend could go.

Ellen, 10th March, 2001. Ellen lives in Warwick in England if she is still alive.

Around this time, a notice was posted asking for volunteers for dress and underwear making, also sewing, cutting, laundry, hairdressing, gardening, handicrafts, carpentry, wood chopping and rubbish collection. Klara was in her element, and within two weeks, there were 1,200 volunteers. Any volunteer could earn tokens to spend in the shops, e.g. 2 tokens a day. 8 tokens were worth 2s 3d. Not a lot in this day and age, but worth having then. There were also English classes, which, to Klara, was manna from Heaven!

The Imperial Hotel was used for the women, and was full of 'high class' prostitutes. Some even had their own maids interned with them. They had plenty of money to spend, with fur coats to wear. At that time, the Golf Links Hotel was full of Nazi women who saluted Heil Hitler to each other in the street. The Hydro Hotel was used as a hospital and had a German woman doctor in charge. There continued to be problems between Nazi and Jewish women, and there was also lots of jealousy, arguing, bickering, and some lesbian relationships blossomed.

Klara did not have any relatives in England, and therefore no one to speak for her, and because of this, she was not finally released from the Isle of Man and internship until December 1942. With nothing but a smattering of English, she returned to London to the charity that had dealt with her all along. Her luggage was shipped after her and paid for by the Charity. It seems the Charity was pressing Klara to have David fostered, and eventually adopted; he went into foster care in August 1942, to a Mrs Bates of Richmond. This happened on his arrival back from release from the Isle of Man. It is clear from the case notes that Klara visited David. But once again, she started the long round of different addresses, and she was in and out of hospitals. She gained the label of 'excitable,' as this is stated at least twice in the case notes. Is it any wonder Klara was 'excitable' having gone through so much, and having David taken from her. The Charity worker alternated between calling Klara Mrs. and Miss.

In 1944, Klara finally succumbed to the pressure, and agreed to have David adopted; there is an entry that shows: 'Miss Stern is anxious for David to have a 'Jewish' upbringing.'

On 18th May 1944, David was taken to Rusthall Beacon Jewish Children's Home in Tunbridge Wells. In the summer of 1947, he went to live with the West-Samuels, and in January 1950 he was legally adopted. He was aged eight at this time.

I think Klara spent some time in a private mental hospital. It is clear that she was depressed – not surprisingly. The saddest entry of all is on 29th April 1946, which states that Klara left Epsom on 24.4.46. with no warning. Destination unknown.

It is clear the charity held on to her luggage until April 1949, when it was destroyed. Questions: Did Klara commit suicide? Were there photos and other things of value to David in the destroyed luggage? There are some things we will never know.

Dora – the feisty one!

Dora was fed up with all the happenings, and in June 1935, she left home at the age of twenty four, going to the nearest big city, which was Frankfurt. Selma and Klara had been so close to each other that she felt like an intruder, and was glad to get away and build an identity for herself. She soon found accommodation and lived quite well, sewing for a job. In her own words, she had three idyllic years without the other sisters.

In May 1938, the sisters joined her in Frankfurt, and told her that her mother was ill and needed her. Not wishing to upset the relationship between Selma and Klara, Dora returned to Gladenbach to nurse her mother, who soon got well again under Dora's tender care. A rich couple who were family friends, asked Dora to return with them to Altenkirchen. Dora was to be the housekeeper and tend to the needs of the elderly couple.

One day, whilst she was living with the elderly couple, three storm-troopers hammered on their door. The couple were very scared and for a while pretended not to be at home. Only after the Storm Troopers pounded the door and broke a window did the elderly man reluctantly open the door. Once inside, the troopers terrorized and beat the two old people. When Dora heard their screams, she came out of her bedroom and standing at the top of the stairs she yelled down, "Why are you doing this? They have done nothing to you. Please, please stop! Don't hurt them anymore. Would you do this to your own grandparents?"

After the three SAs heard Dora's pleas, they stopped beating the elderly couple, whom they had already bound to take them away. The youngest of the soldiers looked Dora in the eye, then looked at the other soldiers, and then left Dora alone. She never saw the couple again. She began to think she was very lucky that they did nothing to her, but did not know why. On recounting this story to others, she said, "God was with me, or I too would have been beaten and taken away."

Dora met and married Ernst Goldsmidt in Altenkirchen. It is not possible to give a date, but it's got to be after February 1939, as Dora returned to Gladenbach for a short time to change her name. The Nazis had decreed that during the early part of 1939, all Jews were to attend their hometown Burgermeister, and officially add 'Sara' to their name if they were a woman, 'Israel' if they were male. This was a good way for the Nazis to know how many Jews there were in Germany, and who they were.

Dora's name change doc

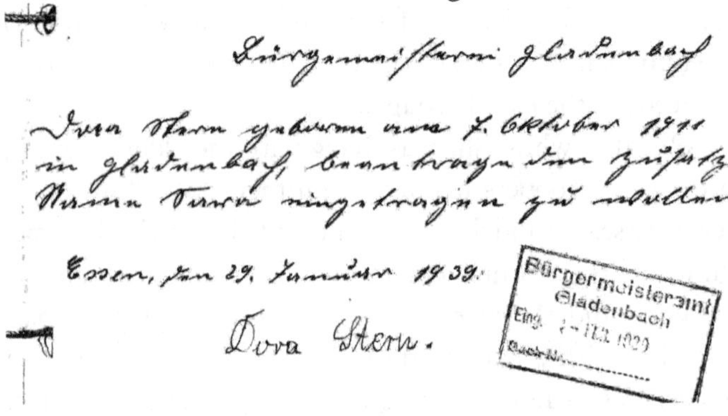
Bürgermeisteramt Gladenbach

Dora Stern geboren am 7. Oktober 1911 in Gladenbach beantrage den Zusatz Namen Sara eingetragen zu wollen

Essen, den 29. Januar 1939.

Dora Stern.

Bürgermeisteramt Gladenbach
Eing.
Buch-Nr.

Ernst was well qualified, as he had a PhD in Agriculture, but he could not get a job in Germany. They were together through Kristallnacht, (attacking and vandalising all that was Jewish) and saw all the terror that it brought, as it happened countrywide. On the night of 9th November, gangs of Nazis roamed Jewish neighbourhoods, breaking the windows of Jewish businesses and homes, burning synagogues, and looting. In all, 101 synagogues and almost 7,500 businesses were destroyed nationwide. What was happening in cities also happened in smaller towns and villages. 26,000 Jews were arrested and sent to concentration camps. Jews were physically attacked and beaten, and ninety-one died.

Ernst was one of the men who were arrested on Kristallnacht for nothing, and sent to hard labour camps. These forced labour camps were, in effect, concentration camps. He was lucky, in that he knew people who were ready to buy him out. In 1939, having spent almost a year away, he came home to Dora.

Kristallnacht turned out to be a turning point in German policy regarding the Jews, and may be considered as the actual beginning of what is now called the Holocaust.

In 1938, the President of the Dominican Republic, who was called Trujillo, opened the immigration doors of his country to Jews, as long as they promised to work on the land. When they heard this in 1939, it sounded ideal for Ernst and Dora. Not only could they escape Germany, they could also pursue Ernst's dream of sensitively turning jungle into liveable land. The president expected newcomers to have the necessary means of support that would keep them from becoming a burden on the receiving state, and in return they were each given a piece of land and a horse. In addition, these newcomers were not to become competition for the local population. Agriculture was practically the only option left open to them, and the Dominican Republic saved the lives of about 3,000 Jewish refugees, merely by granting them a Visa. About 2,000 Jews passed through the Republic before arriving at their final destination, the United States. Trujillo, in tandem with American Jewish organizations, would have welcomed many more refugees, were it not for the lack of funding, and the fact that he wanted immigrants with agricultural skills and knowledge.

The place settled by Jewish immigrants was called Sosúa. This was a small agricultural settlement on the north-eastern shore of the island, where several hundred refugees stayed during the Second World War, as Dominican authorities had granted them asylum. Although the agricultural colony has now vanished, its memory still lives on among the refugees.

In time, Dora became pregnant with her first baby, and they were both thrilled. It was not an easy pregnancy, and where they were, there was no real medical care. The baby was born full term, but died when it was three days old. She never forgave herself for going to the Dominican Republic. She also blamed Ernst, the Nazis, and anyone else she could think of to vent her pain and anger.

It was not so long after this heart-breaking occurrence that Dora announced she wanted to leave and go to the United States. Not many of the Jewish refugees stayed in the Dominican Republic. Most moved to the United States, because it offered them a life more similar to the one they had been forced to leave behind in Europe, and Ernst and Dora were no exception. Only about twenty-five Jewish families remain in Sosúa today, and their dairy businesses supply most of the butter and cheese consumed in the Dominican Republic. There is a saying that Sosúa, a community borne of pain and nurtured in love, must, in the final analysis, represent the ultimate triumph of life.

So in 1940, Ernst and Dora moved to Chicago, because there were family friends there who would help them. Knowing Karl was there, she made contact with him. *Aufbau* was a Jewish weekly newspaper published all over the world, and during and since the war, it has helped people find their long-lost friends and relatives by advertising. Not long after Dora reached Chicago, she read an advertisement that Klara had placed from England in the International *Aufbau*, asking for Dora or Karl to get in touch. The advert said that Klara was trying to find them and wanted to go to the America. It appeared in a box, so Dora knew it must have cost Klara a lot of money. Dora knew where Karl lived and went to see him, taking the advert with her. Karl was furious that Dora had brought him the advert and, without looking at it, ranted about Klara having been pregnant and unmarried and unrepentant when she had left for England. He threatened Dora not to do anything about the advert, and said that in all ways, Klara was dead to him. Dora was afraid of her big brother Karl, and abided by his threats, so did not do anything about the advert and contacting Klara. Klara was never to know that her advert had been seen. Then one day in Chicago, Dora met up with Karl when she got on a bus with a toddler and baby in tow. He completely ignored her, even though she spoke to him, and he pretended he did not know her.

Life moved on, and Dora and Ernst moved to Seattle, where Dora had a third child. Ernst got a job as a baker, and worked until he died, past the retirement age. Having been widowed, Dora lived until she was the grand old age of ninety-six. She was relatively healthy for all of those years, but for the last twenty years of her life, her memory did not serve her well.

The Search

It is said that all research is subjective, in that whosoever collects the information and writes it down, does it entirely to their own set of beliefs. It seemed weirdly right that it should be me to do this research, and it still does. I really don't know where to start, at the beginning I suppose. But, there is no real beginning, as I did not gather information in a chronological order, and it was up to me to piece it altogether as I gathered it, and then to make sense of it. You will remember that I made a pact to give David a sense of who he was, and why he was as he was. Well, that's exactly what I did, but not until his adoptive mother was dead.

From thereon in, the search began. It has taken me almost ten years, but the effort has been worth it. To list out every contact and everything I found would, I think, be somewhat boring, so I won't bother you with those details. You will appreciate that there were many highs and lows, many brick walls, and many leads that amounted to nothing. But all the tears, the laughter, the hopes and the disappointments all came together when a living relative was found. (We had waited until David's adoptive parents had both died.)

In 1979, we were holidaying in the south of England and went through Tunbridge Wells. David vaguely remembered being there as a child, and telephoned his adoptive mother from a phone box. She was very surprised when he spoke to her, asking for the address of the children's home. She said it was all too long ago and that she couldn't remember anything, saying, "Please don't ask me again." With hindsight, at the time she must have talked to David's adoptive father about the phone call, but I remember David being quite upset at the time.

We went to see David's adoptive father quite a lot when his adoptive mother died, especially when he became ill, and one Sunday he produced some very faded, extremely old letters, and a Post Office book which was in David's name. His adoptive father died in 1985 of bowel cancer, and we had both played a great part in nursing him. I have included a copy of these, and you will see that they are dated 1947 to the 60's. After reading the letters, we saved them, along with the Post Office book. I did not really do anything with them, except to keep them safe, but what was contained in these letters was new and useful information.

Letters from David's adopted father

REFUGEE CHILDREN'S MOVEMENT, Ltd.

REGIONAL COMMITTEE No. 9

CHAIRMAN: MISS E. A. BRISTOL.
HON. TREASURER: H. PEARSON, ESQ.
SECRETARY: MISS RUTH J. SIMMONS.
TEL. EDGBASTON 0784

26 CALTHORPE ROAD
EDGBASTON
BIRMINGHAM, 15
5 June 1947

RJS/IH

Mr. & Mrs. Samuel,
"The Firs",
Buildwas Road,
COALBROOKDALE,
Salop.

Dear Mr. and Mrs. Samuel,

Since my visit to you last week-end, I have been "offered" a little boy of 8, who is urgently in need of a home with a view to future adoption. I enclose copy of a report I have received about him and Miss Ney of the Jewish Refugee Committee has given me some further confidential information, which I am now passing on to you, as I feel you should have the full facts of the case before you.

David is the illegitimate child of a Jewish refugee of German origin, who disappeared about a year ago without leaving any trace. He is British born, but cannot be legally adopted at the moment, as it takes 7(seven) years before a death certificate is issued for the mother. However, any family who took him could be made legal guardian and when the seven years are over can legally adopt him. I am told he is a nice, affectionate, lively little boy of average intelligence. Miss Ney knew his mother well. She says she was a little queer, excitable and to her mind a mental borderline case, but this may be due to conditions she had met in life. She was good-hearted and good-natured and the boy certainly does not bear any trace of his mother's peculiarities.

I am going to London on June 18 and will see Miss Ney. If you would like me to have a chat with the boy and to send you my personal opinion, I will try to arrange for him to be brought to London for this purpose.

Do let me know the dates of your own little boy's school holidays and in case you would like to have David on "Trial", we may be able to fix this and I would be pleased to bring him over to you.

I am very anxious to help you to find the right child, as I feel it is a wonderful opportunity for a youngster to share your lovely home

Yours sincerely,

Ruth J. Simmons
Regional Secretary No. 9.

REFUGEE CHILDREN'S MOVEMENT, Ltd.

[redacted]

IN CO-OPERATION WITH THE BIRMINGHAM COUNCIL FOR REFUGEES.

CHAIRMAN: MISS E. A. BRISTOL.
HON. TREASURER: W. VON SIMSON, ESQ.
SECRETARY: MISS RUTH J. SIMMONS.
TEL. EDGBASTON 0784

OFFICE HOURS: 9-30—1.
2-15—5-30.
SATURDAYS BY APPOINTMENT ONLY.

26 CALTHORPE ROAD
EDGBASTON
BIRMINGHAM, 15

RJS/DK

2nd December, 1947

Mr. and Mrs. Samuel,
The Firs, Buildwas Road,
Coalbrokdale, Salop.

Dear Mr. and Mrs. Samuel,

Re: STERN, David.

I have been trying to find out a bit more about David's early background in this country. It seems that David was sent to the All Saints Nursery College, Harrogate when he was 9 months old in 1940. In 1942 he was with his mother in an Internment Camp on the Isle of Man and when Miss Stern was released in May 1943 David was sent to a private Home in Surrey.

I hope this information will give you a further idea of the past. It is not very constructive, I know, but if you want some "research" of a mored etailed nature I will do my best to help you, let me know.

Kind regards
Yours Sincerely,

Ruth Simmons

COPY.

Report on David Stern, born 11.4.39.

David is a healthy and vivid child, affectionate and full of life. He likes to do little jobs and is always willing to help. He gives no trouble in the House, though of course as an active little boy of this age he is sometimes up to mischief.

His schoolteacher confirms that he is an average pupil who needs guiding and sometimes encouraging in his work. He has no outstanding gifts or abilities and fits in all school activities like all normal children. She thinks it would be a blessing to find a home for this child as he is obviously yearning for securit and love.

Rusthall Beacon,
Tunbridge Wells,
Kent,
May 21st '47

(signed) M. Herlitz.

16,Ashton Lane,

S A L E.

Cheshire.

My Ref:
HF/GD/19071.
Your ref:
S.35780/2.

1st August,1956.

Dear Sir,

Re: Klara STERN.

I attach herewith a copy of a letter sent by you on the 8th August,1950, to the Joint Secretary of the Jewish Refugees Committee, 15,Sumner Place, South Kensington,London,S.W.7,and I would appreciate it if you could now give me any definite information regarding the above as some years ago I adopted the son of the above and am most anxious to know whether she is alive or dead.

Awaiting the favour of your reply.

Yours faithfully,

Home Office,
(Aliens Department)
271-277, High Holborn,
London,W.C.1.

RR

Telegraphic Address: Alidep, London
Tel. No.: CHAncery 8811

Ext.

Any communication on the subject of this letter should be addressed to :—
THE UNDER SECRETARY OF STATE

And the following number quoted:
S.35780/2

Your reference RF/GD/19071

HOME OFFICE,
ALIENS DEPARTMENT,
PRINCETON HOUSE,
271 7, HIGH HOLBORN,
LONDON, W.C.1

11th September, 1956.

Sir,

<u>Klara Stern</u>

I am directed by the Secretary of State to refer to your letter of 1st August and to say that he regrets he has not been able to obtain any further information in regard to Mrs. Stern.

I am, Sir,
Your obedient Servant,

E. R. Ballard

Mr. W. Samuel,
16, Ashton Lane,
Sale,
Cheshire.

MB

Post Office Savings Department
Blythe Road
LONDON. W.14.

Telephone: 01-603 2000
Telex: 21212

Your reference

17th February, 1967.

Our reference
14128.S.67/D.C.B.26A.

Dear Mr. West-Samuel,

I thank you for your letter of the 11th January and note what you say.

I have to explain, however, that in the absence of documentary evidence of the death of Mrs. K. Stern, the moneys in her account "Willesden High Rd. 78 Number 12813" must remain deposited in her name.

Yours truly,

for Director of Savings.

Mr. M. West-Samuel,
224, Washway Road,
SALE, Cheshire.

It was in 1984, I was appointed Head of a Counselling Service for the then National Children's Home in Preston, and I spoke to a colleague about my intended research. She advised me to talk to David and if he was willing, to get a copy of his original Birth Certificate. David made an application to the Social Services that covered the area and they sent a male social worker to 'counsel' him. When this man saw that David was serious, he arranged for a copy birth certificate. When the Certificate arrived, we were able to see not only the name of his birth mother, but where he was born, as well as a few other pieces of information.

David's birth certificate

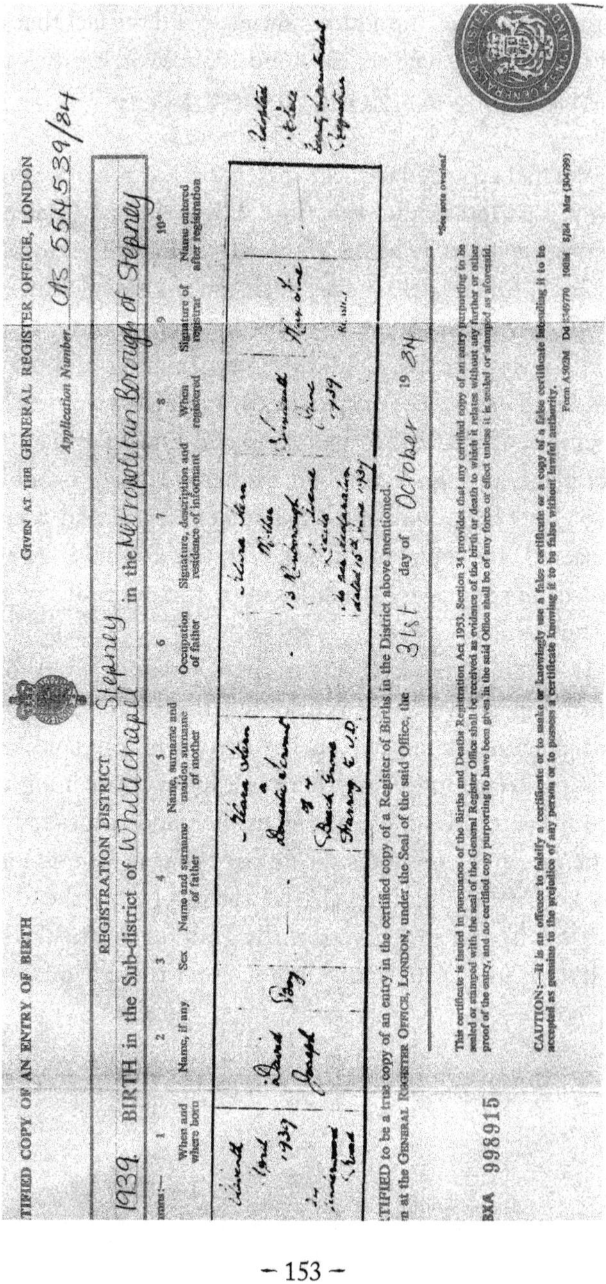
TIFIED COPY OF AN ENTRY OF BIRTH

GIVEN AT THE GENERAL REGISTER OFFICE, LONDON

Application Number CAS 554539/84

REGISTRATION DISTRICT Stepney

1939. BIRTH in the Sub-district of Whitechapel in the Metropolitan Borough of Stepney

Columns:— 1 When and where born	2 Name, if any	3 Sex	4 Name and surname of father	5 Name, surname and maiden surname of mother	6 Occupation of father	7 Signature, description and residence of informant	8 When registered	9 Signature of registrar	10* Name entered after registration
[illegible] 1939	David Joseph	Boy	—	Clara [illegible] a Domestic Servant	—	Clara [illegible] Mother 13 [illegible] Avenue Leeds	June 1939	[illegible] Registrar	[illegible]

TIFIED to be a true copy of an entry in the certified copy of a Register of Births in the District above mentioned.

n at the GENERAL REGISTER OFFICE, LONDON, under the Seal of the said Office, the 31st day of October 1984

*See note overleaf

BXA 998915

This certificate is issued in pursuance of the Births and Deaths Registration Act 1953. Section 34 provides that any certified copy of an entry purporting to be sealed or stamped with the seal of the General Register Office shall be received as evidence of the birth or death to which it relates without any further or other proof of the entry, and no certified copy purporting to have been given in the said Office shall be of any force or effect unless it is sealed or stamped as aforesaid.

CAUTION:—It is an offence to falsify a certificate or to make or knowingly use a false certificate or a copy of a false certificate intending it to be accepted as genuine to the prejudice of any person or to possess a certificate knowing it to be false without lawful authority.

Form A502M Dd 8349770 100M 8/84 Mcr (304799)

On it, there was the address of the place he was born, his mother's name, the address she gave and the fact that she had registered David on 15th June 1939. We already knew most of this information from the letters.

We had arranged to meet with my eldest son in Bethnal Green, London around this time. His girlfriend (Helen at the time) took us to where the Jewish Maternity Hospital was in Whitechapel. It was such an emotional time for David, to walk, as it were, in his mother's footsteps. The building was the only building left standing and David went in. It was no longer specifically for Jewish women, but a member of staff confirmed to David that he was in the right place, and she remembered it being Jewish! I couldn't believe our luck, and said so. I remember, David was so emotional, he could not speak. I knew I would have to leave things alone for a while, until the enormity of the visit sunk in.

In 1985, I tracked down the Charity CBF World Jewish Relief, which had absorbed the original Charity dealing with his mother on her arrival in England, and during the ensuing War. There is a letter confirming our appointment in London, giving us the opportunity to look at the original case notes. So off we went to London and duly kept the appointment. This was just before the Open Access Act, and so we were really grateful to the Charity for letting us see these case notes, even though we could not have a copy.

LETTER FROM CBF WJR

CBF World Jewish Relief

Drayton House · Gordon Street · London WC1H 0AN
Tel 01-387 3925/3979/5461 Cble Migrate London WC1

13th May 1985

Mrs. Tina West-Samuel
7 Lower Dolphinholme
Lancaster
LA2 9AX

Dear Mrs. West-Samuel,

This is to confirm an appointment for your husband to come and see us on Tuesday 21st May at about 2.30 pm, as asked by your letter of 10th May 1985, addressed to Mrs. Nissan.

Please note our new address, as above.

Yours sincerely,

Michele Williams
Secretary - Jewish Refugees Committee

MW/RN

I underestimated the emotional impact that this would have on David. To see his own mother referred to as 'the woman' and to read comments about the clothing given for 'the baby' was just awful for him. She had clearly acquired the label of 'excitable' from the social workers who dealt with her at the time. I frantically made some notes of names and addresses where Klara was known to have been. It seemed she moved around a lot in those war torn years. Just after our visit, David received a letter from the Secretary of the Jewish Refugee Committee. She said that a woman who was mentioned in the case notes as Miss Ruth Simmonds, was now a Mrs. Wolfe. Mrs. Wolfe had told the secretary that she did not remember 'the case,' but she would be happy to talk on the telephone or in person. A full address was given for Mrs. Wolfe, and she lived in Birmingham.

Also, in 1985 I wrote to 'Germania Judaica' to see if anyone there could help me. I received a very nice letter back from Dr. Monika Richarz; she had been talking about my letter to a German Historian, Raymond Wolff, who gave some very sound advice. I am afraid that the gap I left in the time between receiving this letter from the Jewish Charity, and my contacting Mrs. Wolfe, was left just too long, because when I finally contacted the address, I was told that unfortunately, Mrs. Wolfe had died in the meantime.

Letter from Germania Judecia

Raymond Wolff

Wildenbruchplatz 4
1000 Berlin 44
West Germany

Mr. David J. West Samuel
7 Lower Dolphinholme
Lancaster LA2 9AX
England

Köln, den 8. Juli 1985

Dear Mr. Samuel,

I am a German-Jewish historian from Berlin who is spending a few days in Köln visiting my good friend, the directrice of the Germania Judaica library, Dr. Monika Richarz. She showed me your letter and I thought I would write you and give you advice.

First of all, there is a newspaper which comes out twice a month called "Aufbau". It is published in New York City and is read by many many Jewish emigrants from Germany all over the world. It is "the" German-Jewish paper. Practically every week there are advertisements (which must be paid for) put in by people looking for other people. You could do this for your mother, puting in her name and place of birth. The "Aufbau" is so widely read in these circles that something or other should come from such an advert. The address of the newspaper (you must ask for their price list) is: Aufbau
2121 Broadway
New York,
New York 10023
U.S.A.

Now for my next bit of advice. You mention that your mother was "apparently" born in Gladenbach. If this is so--- several years back I saw a television show about a man, a Jew, who returned to his home town after the war and is today the only Jew living there. This man is from and is living in (if he hasn't died in the meanwhile) Gladenbach!! I don't remember his name, but tomorrow morning, before I mail off this letter, I will call the city hall in Gladenbach and see if I can get this man's address for you. It is, however, doubtful if he speaks english, so you should have someone write a letter to him in German. Since Gladenbach isn't that big (I've been there), I am sure all the Jews there knew one another. He might also know about other relative of youre.

Your mother's birth certificate would be in the "Standesamt" (civil records office) in the "Rathaus" (city hall) of Gladenbach as all records (births, deaths, marriages) on your family in Gladenbach would be.

-2-

Only after the sources in the city hall are exhausted and if you are interested, for curiosities sake, to trace your family back a bit further, the birth, death and marriage records of the Jewish inhabitants of Gladenbach are kept in the Hessisches Hauptstaats-archiv (the main state archives for the state of Hessen) in Wiesbaden. The address of this archive plus the information I promised you on page 1 I will type on to this letter tomorrow. I sincerely hope that this information will be of use to you.

Sincerely,

Raymond Wolff

I just called up Gladenbach. I'm sorry to say that the Jewish man has died in the meantime. But, like I wrote, the civil records of Gladenbach should help you. It would be best if you go there yourself, but if you can't, write them and tell them what you want.

The address is: Standesamt Gladenbach
Rathaus
3568 Gladenbach
West Germany

The telephone number is: 49 (06462) 2010

The area

the coun

The addr

Good Lu

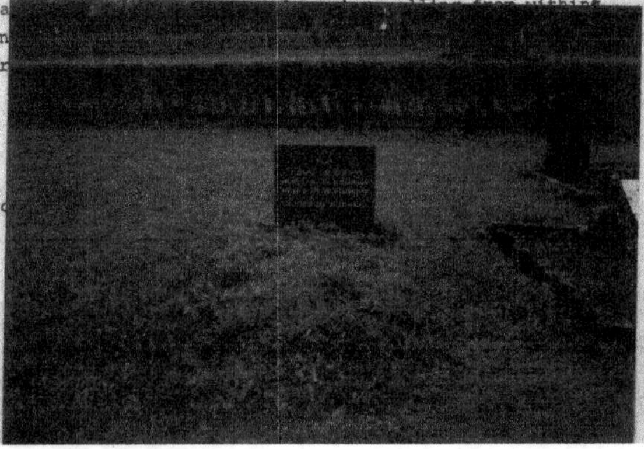

In 1986 I wrote a letter to the DHSS (Department of Health and Social Security, as it was named then), my thinking being that if Klara was still in England, she would be getting a Pension now and they might have records on her. They wrote back that it was not possible to find any records.

1986 also saw me write to the Post Office to try and reclaim the money that Klara had meant for David. (It is worth noting the last deposit in the book.) If I could get the money, I had a very real use for it. The saddest part of this story is that the savings book was not in Klara's name - it was named, 'for David Stern'. She had signed the book to this effect, and this was Klara's legacy to her son. There is one special story contained within the case notes that I have pieced together, which I feel should not go untold.

From the summer of 1945 onwards, Klara was alone and was having trouble with her teeth. She was referred to a dentist. Remember at that time there was no National Health Service and all treatment had to be paid for. From the case notes, it seems she had to go for an examination and get an estimate of the cost of dental treatment and then request the money from the Charity who dealt with her. All this before any treatment could take place, because in those days, dentists wanted the money before the treatment. When you match the costs with the amount she earned you can see how expensive it was, as the very last estimate was the relatively very large sum of £6.7s 6d. I am led to believe that Klara was given this last sum of money, but never actually had the treatment, and was probably in great pain, only adding to her feelings of desperation.

Why did Klara never make that final visit to the dentist? The question I have is, who in their right mind would leave everything they had and just disappear?

Post office book

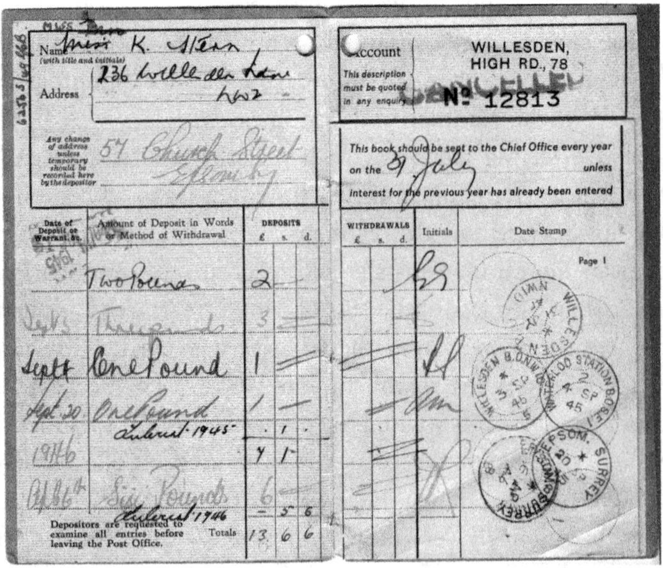

Name (with title and initials) Miss K. Stern

Address 236 Willesden Lane NW2

Any change of address unless temporary should be recorded here by the depositor 57 Church Street

Account WILLESDEN, HIGH RD., 78

This description must be quoted in any enquiry

CANCELLED

Nº 12813

This book should be sent to the Chief Office every year on the 29 July unless interest for the previous year has already been entered

Date of Deposit or Warrant, &c.	Amount of Deposit in Words or Method of Withdrawal	DEPOSITS £	s.	d.	WITHDRAWALS £	s.	d.	Initials	Date Stamp
1945	Two Pounds	2							Page 1
	Three Pounds	3							
Sept	One Pound	1							
Sept 20	One Pound	1							
	Interest 1945		1						
1946		7	1						
	Six Pounds	6							
	Interest 1946		5	6					
Depositors are requested to examine all entries before leaving the Post Office.	Totals	13	6	6					

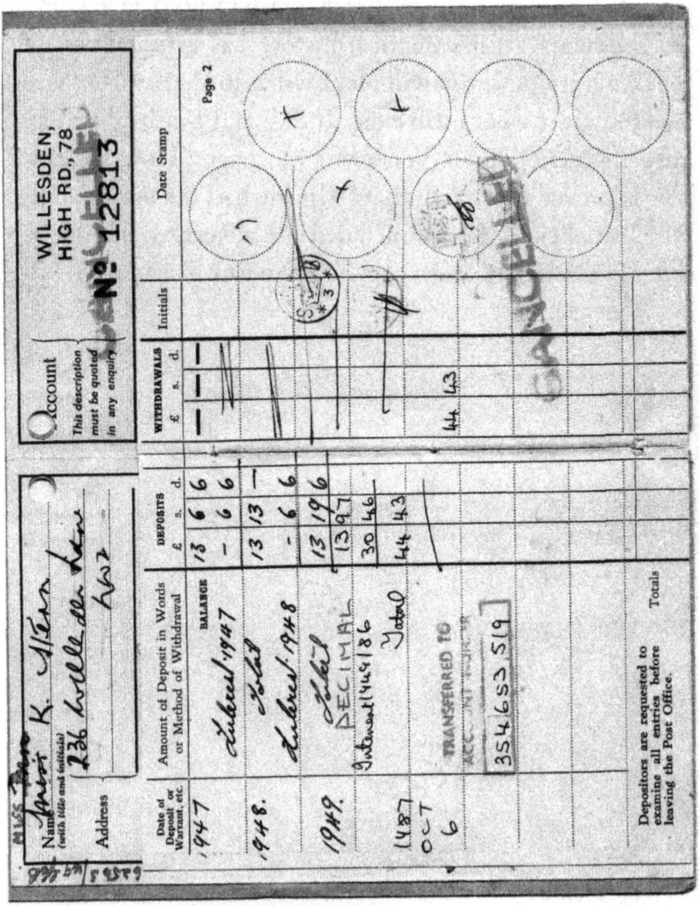
WILLESDEN, HIGH RD., 78
Nº 12813
Account
This description must be quoted in any enquiry
Name (with title and initials) Miss K. Alter
Address 236 Willesden Lane NW2
Page 2

Date of Deposit or Warrant, etc.	Amount of Deposit in Words or Method of Withdrawal	Deposits £	s.	d.	Withdrawals £	s.	d.	Initials	Date Stamp
	BALANCE								
1947	Interest 1947	13	6	6	—	—	—		
		—	6	6					
1948	Total	13	13	—					
	Interest 1948	—	6	6					
1949	Total	13	19	6					
	DECIMAL	13.97							
	Interest 1949/86	30.46							
14.8.7 OCT 6	Total	44.43			44.43				
	TRANSFERRED TO ACCOUNT NUMBER 354653 519								
	Totals								

Depositors are requested to examine all entries before leaving the Post Office.

CANCELLED

It was only later, knowing and understanding this information, we decided to apply to the Post Office for the return of the money, as we had a very special use for it. That small sum of money had, over the years, accrued a lot of interest and David was paid over £40!

We poignantly used the money to pay for the advertisement in 'Aufbau,' in our search for Klara. This was the same newspaper that Klara had used to try and track down Karl in America; history has a funny way of repeating itself, as you will see. I wrote to 'Aufbau' because I just knew it would still exist. It did, and I duly placed an advertisement in their 'Where are you' pages. However, this advert proved useless, in that I already had the information which it elicited. I have included the advert, copies of the letters to 'Aufbau,' and a copy of the post office book.

Letter and advert from Aufbau

0101
TEL. (212) 873-7400

AUFBAU

CABLE ADDRESS:
"AUFBAU" NEW YORK

A DIVISION OF NEW WORLD CLUB INC.

AMERICA'S LEADING GERMAN LANGUAGE NEWSPAPER

2121 BROADWAY • NEW YORK, N.Y. 10023

April 2, 1986

Mr. and Mrs. David West-Samuel
7 Lower Dolphin Holme
Lancaster LA2 9AX
England

Dear Mr. and Mrs. West-Samuel:

Thank you for your inquiry for search ads.

We do put ads for searches for relatives in our paper.

Any information you may have - birthplace and date, maiden and married name (names of parents if known), when she left Germany to go where. If you have any other brothers and sisters, mention their names. Include your mother's address before she left Germany. The same information (if available) about any relatives you are looking for. Enclosed are different sizes and prices. Should your message be bigger, size and price will go up.

Hoping to hear from you soon, we remain,

With kind regards,

Ida Sternberg
Ida Sternberg
Advertising Manager

IS:mt
Encl.

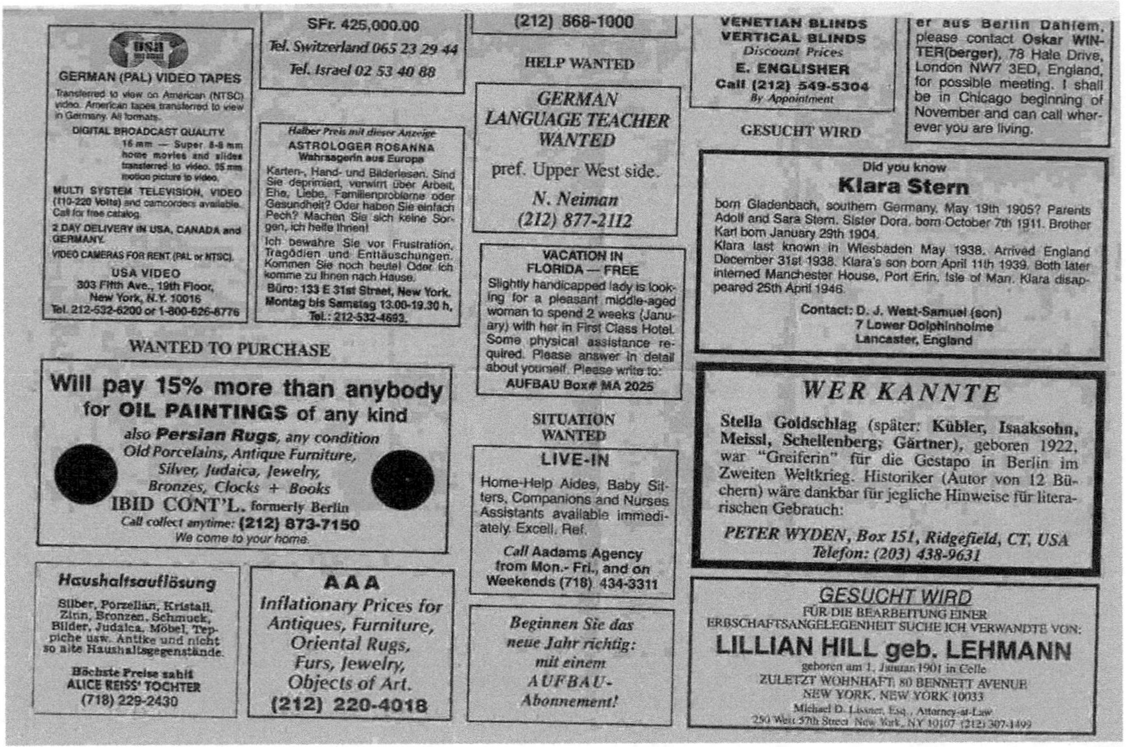
GERMAN (PAL) VIDEO TAPES
Transferred to view on American (NTSC) video. American tapes transferred to view in Germany. All formats.
DIGITAL BROADCAST QUALITY.
16 mm — Super 8-8 mm home movies and slides transferred to video. 35 mm motion picture to video.
MULTI SYSTEM TELEVISION, VIDEO (110-220 Volts) and camcorders available. Call for free catalog.
2 DAY DELIVERY IN USA, CANADA and GERMANY.
VIDEO CAMERAS FOR RENT (PAL or NTSC).
USA VIDEO
303 Fifth Ave., 19th Floor, New York, N.Y. 10016
Tel. 212-532-6200 or 1-800-626-8776
SFr. 425,000.00
Tel. Switzerland 065 23 29 44
Tel. Israel 02 53 40 88
Halber Preis mit dieser Anzeige
ASTROLOGER ROSANNA
Wahrsagerin aus Europa
Karten-, Hand- und Bilderlesen. Sind Sie deprimiert, verwirrt über Arbeit, Ehe, Liebe, Familienprobleme oder Gesundheit? Oder haben Sie einfach Pech? Machen Sie sich keine Sorgen, ich helfe Ihnen!
Ich bewahre Sie vor Frustration, Tragödien und Enttäuschungen. Kommen Sie noch heute! Oder ich komme zu Ihnen nach Hause.
Büro: 133 E 31st Street, New York. Montag bis Samstag 13.00-19.30 h, Tel.: 212-532-4693.
WANTED TO PURCHASE
Will pay 15% more than anybody for OIL PAINTINGS of any kind
also Persian Rugs, any condition
Old Porcelains, Antique Furniture, Silver, Judaica, Jewelry, Bronzes, Clocks + Books
IBID CONT'L. formerly Berlin
Call collect anytime: (212) 873-7150
We come to your home.
Haushaltsauflösung
Silber, Porzellan, Kristall, Zinn, Bronzen, Schmuck, Bilder, Judaica, Möbel, Teppiche usw. Antike und nicht so alte Haushaltsgegenstände.
Höchste Preise zahlt
ALICE REISS' TOCHTER
(718) 229-2430
AAA
Inflationary Prices for Antiques, Furniture, Oriental Rugs, Furs, Jewelry, Objects of Art.
(212) 220-4018
(212) 868-1000
HELP WANTED
GERMAN LANGUAGE TEACHER WANTED
pref. Upper West side.
N. Neiman
(212) 877-2112
VACATION IN FLORIDA — FREE
Slightly handicapped lady is looking for a pleasant middle-aged woman to spend 2 weeks (January) with her in First Class Hotel. Some physical assistance required. Please answer in detail about yourself. Please write to:
AUFBAU Box# MA 2025
SITUATION WANTED
LIVE-IN
Home-Help Aides, Baby Sitters, Companions and Nurses Assistants available immediately. Excell. Ref.
Call Aadams Agency from Mon.- Fri., and on Weekends (718) 434-3311
Beginnen Sie das neue Jahr richtig: mit einem AUFBAU-Abonnement!
VENETIAN BLINDS
VERTICAL BLINDS
Discount Prices
E. ENGLISHER
Call (212) 549-5304
By Appointment
GESUCHT WIRD
er aus Berlin Dahlem, please contact Oskar WINTER(berger), 78 Hale Drive, London NW7 3ED, England, for possible meeting. I shall be in Chicago beginning of November and can call wherever you are living.
Did you know
Klara Stern
born Gladenbach, southern Germany, May 19th 1905? Parents Adolf and Sara Stern. Sister Dora, born October 7th 1911. Brother Karl born January 29th 1904.
Klara last known in Wiesbaden May 1938. Arrived England December 31st 1938. Klara's son born April 11th 1939. Both later interned Manchester House, Port Erin, Isle of Man. Klara disappeared 25th April 1946.
Contact: D. J. West-Samuel (son)
7 Lower Dolphinholme
Lancaster, England
WER KANNTE
Stella Goldschlag (später: Kübler, Isaaksohn, Meissl, Schellenberg; Gärtner), geboren 1922, war "Greiferin" für die Gestapo in Berlin im Zweiten Weltkrieg. Historiker (Autor von 12 Büchern) wäre dankbar für jegliche Hinweise für literarischen Gebrauch:
PETER WYDEN, Box 151, Ridgefield, CT, USA
Telefon: (203) 438-9631
GESUCHT WIRD
FÜR DIE BEARBEITUNG EINER ERBSCHAFTSANGELEGENHEIT SUCHE ICH VERWANDTE VON:
LILLIAN HILL geb. LEHMANN
geboren am 1. Januar 1901 in Celle
ZULETZT WOHNHAFT: 80 BENNETT AVENUE
NEW YORK, NEW YORK 10033
Michael D. Lissner, Esq., Attorney-at-Law
250 West 57th Street New York, NY 10107 (212) 307-1499

On photocopying everything I had, I realised that many of the letters were as though David was writing them, so the replies are addressed to him. I thought I would be sure of an answer this way!

In March 1986, I wrote to the Town Hall in Gladenbach to ask if they could tell me what had happened to Klara and the family. It was nearly a month before they replied, with news I already knew, except that Dora had married in a place called Gelsenkirchen.

By 1989, I was still as determined as ever to find out about David's history, and could think of nothing else. In 1989, it was fifty years since David had been born. I decided I was going to surprise him and take him to Germany, to the village where Klara was born. I contacted his employer, got permission for him to be away from work for three days, and my eldest son took us to the airport. The night before, I told David that I was taking him to the airport for breakfast and a look around. He did not think this was strange as he was mad about planes and airports at the time. I managed to pack a bag and put it in the car without him knowing, and in the morning we set off to what David thought would be a 'flying' visit. He was so surprised he could not speak.

Our arrival at Frankfurt airport was uneventful, except in the city we witnessed a young people's pro-Nazi demonstration; there were many steel barriers up, and a heavy police presence. I understand that nowadays this kind of demonstration would be illegal. The two of us left quickly to find the local train station. This was fun, as David doesn't really have a word of German, and I only had school German. It got us by anyway, when I went to book two tickets for Gladenbach. It turned out to be a two carriage, mountain train that left on time and arrived on time! The scenery from Frankfurt to Gladenbach was beautiful, and Gladenbach station was tiny and rural. We set off to walk to the village, and I remember that the streets were lined with Magnolia trees, all in blossom. I remember I commented on this.

On reaching the village/town we made a beeline for the Town Hall, as I thought we would stand a good chance of gaining information there. People there were very helpful, and from the minute we arrived, it seemed there was a guiding hand.

Letter and translation from Gladenbach Town Hall

STADT GLADENBACH

KNEIPP-HEILBAD

DER MAGISTRAT

Stadt Gladenbach · Postfach 1240 · 3554 Gladenbach

Frau
Tina Samuel
1 Lower Dolphinholme

Lancaster LAZ 9AX
England

Amt
Standesamt

Ringstraße 34

Auskunft erteilt
Herr Happel

Zimmer-Nr.
115

Vermittlung
0 64 62/201-0

Durchwahl
201- 131

Sprechstunden: Montag bis Freitag von 8.30 – 12.30 Uhr
Donnerstag von 14.00 – 17.30 Uhr

Bankverbindungen:
Kreissparkasse Gladenbach (BLZ 517 520 66) 101 011.5
Volksbank Gladenbach (BLZ 517 623 34) 50 527 000
Postscheckkonto Frankfurt/Main 149 02-608

Ihr Schreiben	Ihr Zeichen	Unser Zeichen	3554 Gladenbach, den
v. 24.03.1986		III A-052-51-Hp/Schd	10. April 1986

Sehr geehrte Frau Samuel!

Leider konnten wir Ihren Brief erst heute beantworten, da eine Übersetzung nötig war und auch Unterlagen aus dem Archiv beigebracht werden mußten.

Aus den hier vorhandenen Dokumenten ist zu ersehen, daß Klara Stern am 16.05.1905 in Gladenbach geboren ist, ebenso ihre Schwester Dora Stern am 07.10.1911 in Gladenbach, die im Jahre 1939 unter Nr. 1716 beim Standesamt in Gelsenkirchen geheiratet hat. Der Name des Ehemannes ist nicht bekannt. Die Namen der Eltern lauten, Adolf Stern von Beruf Metzger und Sarah Stern geborene Stern, beide israelitischer Religion.

Als weiterer Anhaltspunkt über die Familie Stern können wir nur die Angaben machen, die aus beiliegender Aufstellung zu ersehen sind. Diese Aufstellung ist aus einem Dokument ehemaliger jüdischer Bürger aus Gladenbach.

Wir bedauern, Ihnen keine weiteren Ausführungen machen zu können.

Mit freundlichen Grüßen

Happel

Happel
Standesbeamter

On entering, I explained why we were there and the person who I spoke to said to wait one minute. He left us and returned quickly with Heinrich, who spoke really good English. He explained that he had been stationed in Wales whilst he was in the Army, and was married to a Welsh girl, hence the good English. Later on, they were to visit us in our small cottage in Lancashire, and we have kept in touch with Heinrich through the years.

As we were explaining to Heinrich why we were there, he said, "Just a minute!" and ran off to stop a man called Jurgen Rundsheimer from leaving the Town Hall. Later, Heinrich took us in his car to the house where the Stern's had lived, the Jewish graveyard, so that we could view David's great-grandparents' grave, and on to Marburg, the nearest town. Marburg was a University town, but had been where the Grimm Brothers had written their fairy tales.

In Marburg, all the houses were made of black and white timber, just how we had imagined it. Heinrich made us so welcome, and took us home with him to meet his wife and for an evening meal. Again, we were so grateful to have met someone who understood what we were doing, and the reasons behind our search. We slept in a pub/chalet/B+B that night, and went back to Frankfurt the next day with promises to keep in touch with Heinrich and his wife. We got home feeling we had achieved what we set out to do, and there was a big party at the local village hall to celebrate David's fiftieth birthday. A good time was had by all!

LITERAL TRANSLATION.

Very worthy Mrs. Samuel!

Unfortunately we were unable to answer your letter straight away as a translation was necessary and also a search through the archives.

From the documents in our possession, Klara Stern was born 16.05.1905 in Gladenback, as was her sister Dora on 7.10.1911, who in fact married in 1939 under the number 1716 in Gelsenkirchen. The name of her husband is not known. The names of the parents were, according to Adolf Stern .... as letter ... They were both of Isreali Religion.

We can find no further clues about the Stern family. We can only state that from the accompanying information we can learn nothing more. The statement was from a document of a former Jewish Citizen in Gladenbach.

We are sorry we are unable to supply any further information.

With friendly greetings.

JURGEN RUNDSHEIMER

Jurgen Rundsheimer

The man, Jurgen Rundsheimer, had turned back with Heinrich, who told us he had left Gladenbach during the war, and was now a retired Headmaster of the local school. He had vowed that he was going to find out about what had happened to every Jew who had left Gladenbach during the war. (Talk about serendipity!) He was very pleased to see us, and told us that he had made himself a 'historian' since retirement, and was determined to document what had happened to all the Jews who used to live in Gladenbach before 1939. He actually published a book much later on, and sent me a copy, but because it was in German, I have been unable to read it.

As you can imagine, we spent much time talking to him. He left, promising to write to us in England when he had some information. Over the years, Jurgen proved to be a mine of information, and he and I were in regular contact. Sadly, he died in 2012, but as late as 2007, he wrote to me.

During 1987, somewhat disappointed that it seemed I would never find out more, I wrote to the International Tracing Service of the Red Cross. It would be four years before I heard anything worth knowing from them. All in all, I did not hold out too much hope. That was in 1989, and it was not until November 1989 that I received a letter from Jurgen, complete with a copy of The Stern Family Tree dating back to 1777, that I got really interested again. David too, was very interested, as Jurgen had produced a wealth of information for us, going all the way back to 1775.

Stern Family History

THE STERN FAMILY TREE

Compiled by Jurgen Runzheimer in Gladenbach from records held at the Town Hall there:

Great-Great-Great Grandparents:

Wolf Liebmann (Wolf son of Liebmann) was born some time around 1750
In 1775 he was accepted on to the register of Jewish patrons.
In 1777 he already had a property in Gladenbach consisting of a house and stabling. Its insurable value was 800 guilders.
On 3.3.1809 Wolf Liebmann adopted the surname of Stern
Wolf married a woman called Esther. This would have been before 1789 as their youngest child was born on 2.7.1789. I have no records of other children but there were as it is recorded that:
on his death in 1830 and his children inherited the house.

Great-Great Grandparents:

Abraham was born 2.7.1789. He was the youngest son of Wolf Stern.
Abraham led a very unusual life. He served 6 years in the Archducal Light Cavalry Regiment "Chevaux Legers". After his demobilisation in 1823 he converted to the Christian Religion and renamed himself Christian Reinhard, after his Godfather. He became a second hand and trinket dealer.
In 1824 he married Anna Katharina Lang. This marriage soon ended in divorce, after which he converted back to his former name and Judaism.
In 1829 Abraham applied for, and was refused by the Town council, Citizenship of Gladenbach. He gave the reason as his betrothal to Esther, daughter of the Jewish patron Wolf. Abraham lodged a complaint with the District Council in Biedenkopf, outlining his curriculum vitae and his assets, which amounted to 8,000 guilders - a considerable sum of money relative to those times. The District council ordered reports from the town council and expressed its indignation at the refusal. There is no further documentation.
In 1830 Abraham married Esther Wolf in a Jewish ceremony.
It is not known what happened but in 1832 he married Greila Elias the mother of his son Simon.
In 1834 Abraham applied for citizenship of Romerhausen (the birthplace of his first wife). He wished to move there with his second wife. At that

time he was listed as an apprentice (I don't know what of). There is a document showing his Prussian nationality. He apparently remained in Gladenbach after all.
On 13.4.1838 the official doctor (Dr. Deibel) confirmed the death of Abraham's wife.
Abraham married once more. Her name was Amalie. Amalie is recorded as still being alive in 1900 and is entered in the records as Grandmother Amalie Stern.

Great-Grandparents:

Simon was Abraham's son and was born on 24.1.1833. It is not known if there were brothers and sisters. He married Jettchen Rosenberg (born 24.5.1840) in 1874. Jettchen's parents lived in Grossenbuseck. Her father was a butcher.
Simon and Jettchen were listed as second hand dealers in Gladenbach.
Simon and Jettchen had 3 children who were Lina, Adolf and Sally.
Simon died before Jettchen in 1907. When he died they had been married 33 years. Jettchen died 15.10.1912
They are both buried in the same grave in the Jewish cemetery in Gladenbach. David and I have seen the gravestone.

Grandparents:

Sisters:
Lina was born 28.3.1872 Not much is known about her except that she was recorded as still living with her mother in 1911. According to Aunt Dora, Lina became a midwife and was very good at what she did.
Sally was born 11.1.1875 and there are no further traces on record.

Grandfather:

Adolf was the middle child born 3.6.1873. He married Sarah (born 10.10.1873 sometime around 1900. Prior to marriage Sarah was also called Stern. This is not unusual as there were 5 families named Stern in Gladenbach at that time and it was a common name elsewhere. It is thought they married somewhere else, as the marriage is not recorded in Gladenbach. Sarah came from Neustadt so they may have married there. Adolf is listed in town records as a tradesman butcher.

It was in 1990, when the Berlin Wall came down, that Jurgen again contacted us with more news about David's family. He said it was easier now to get photocopies and proof from the East of Germany. He had found out that Adolph and Sarah had died in a concentration camp, and that Karl had gone to America. He asked me for Power of Attorney as far as release of information went, I granted this, signed the form and hey presto, in 1993, two death certificates arrived from Theresienstadt, Adolph and Sarah's.

In 1991, I wrote to Mrs. Wolfe who had been recommended years before as a possible source of information, but as I have already said, she had died a few years before. All this time I thought the search was taking too long, and so lost interest.

I also wrote to the British Immigration Service in January 1991, and got a little information that I already knew; however, I did get some additional information about Klara's internment on the Isle of Man being May 1940 to December 1942. From what little I knew of internees, this sounded an awfully long time. At the same time, I wrote to the CBF World Jewish Relief as the 'Open Access' law had been passed, and I wanted copies of the original case notes, if at all possible. At a cost of £25 they were duly sent to me. (See photocopies of original case notes and my attempt at deciphering them earlier.)

In 1993, I heard again from the International Tracing Service; their letter told me of the deaths of Adolph and Sarah, but also that Selma had died in Stuttof Concentration Camp in December 1944. This was the first time I'd had news of Selma, and this spurred me on to learn as much as I could about Stutthof Camp. It did not make pleasant reading. As I put the survivor accounts in with 'Selma' and what happened to her, I think you will agree.

In June of 1994, a letter arrived telling us that Dora, (Adolph and Sarah's youngest daughter, who is now 83,) was alive and well and living in Seattle, U.S.A.

Letter from Red Cross

SERVICE INTERNATIONAL DE RECHERCHES
INTERNATIONAL TRACING SERVICE
INTERNATIONALER SUCHDIENST

COMITE INTERNATIONAL GENEVE

D - 3548 AROLSEN
Tel. (05691) 6037 · Telegr.-Adr. ITS Arolsen

Arolsen, 13th October 19
IH/wa

Mr David Joseph West-Samuel
7 Lower Dolphenholme

Dolphierholme, Lancaster LA2 9AX

England

Re: Ascertainment of the whereabouts of
Mrs Klara STERN, born on 16.5.1905

Dear Mr West-Samuel,

In reply to your letter which arrived here on 21st August 1987 we must advise you that the International Tracing Service may only carry out investigations to locate persons if they belong to one of the groups about whom we hold records.

For details please see the attached leaflet informing you about our scope of activity and available documentary material.

We return your letter and recommend that you contact the followi institution, indicating your family relationship to Mrs Klara Stern:

The British Red Cross Society
9 Grosvenor Crescent

London, SW1X 7EJ

With kind regards,

F. Fl
for the Archives

Enclosures: 2

SERVICE INTERNATIONAL DE RECHERCHES
INTERNATIONAL TRACING SERVICE
INTERNATIONALER SUCHDIENST

Arolsen, 21st October 1993
My/ks

Mr David Joseph West-Samuel
7 Lower Dolphinholme

Lancaster LAZ 9AX

England

Our Reference
(please quote)
T/D - 582 546

Re: Your request concerning your grandparents,
Mr Adolf STERN, born on 3.6.1873,
Mrs Sara STERN, born on 12.10.1873, as well as your further relatives, Mrs Selma STERN, born on 19.7.1902, Mr Karl STERN, born in Gladenbach on 27.1.1904 and Mrs Dora STERN, born in Gladenbach on 17.10.1911

Dear Mr West-Samuel,

Reference is made to your letters dated 10th May 1990 and 10th January 1992, as well as your communication, which arrived here on 24th July 1992. We also refer to our letters dated 5th July 1990 and 22nd June 1992.

Please be advised that based on the particulars which you gave, a check was made of the documentary material at our disposal.

As result of our investigations we herewith enclose Excerpts from Documents, which contain all the information on hand here about the incarceration and, sadly, also about the death of Mrs Sara STERN Mr Adolf STERN.

Enclosed are also Extracts of the register of deaths, issued by the Special Registry Office Arolsen.

Furthermore, the additional information could be taken from our available records:

./.

Grosse Allee 5 - 9, 34444 AROLSEN, Bundesrepublik Deutschland, Tel. (0 56 91) 60 37, Telegr. ITS Arolsen

SERVICE INTERNATIONAL DE RECHERCHES
INTERNATIONAL TRACING SERVICE
INTERNATIONALER SUCHDIENST

Arolsen, 9th June 1994
hi/ks

Mr David Joseph West-Samuel
7 Lower Dolphinholme

Lancaster LAZ 9AX

England

Our Reference
(please quote)
T/D - 1 428 799

Re: Mr Karl STERN, born in Gladenbach on 27.1.1904 and
Mrs Dora STERN, born in Gladenbach on 17.10.1911

Dear Mr West-Samuel,

We revert to our letter dated 21st October 1993 and inform you that Mrs Dora STERN married SMIDT could be located and advised of your tracing request.

From the office working together with us, we were informed that Mrs Smidt does not recognize the inquirer's name. However, she is very interested to make contact with you. The address is as follows:

Mrs Dora Smidt
14337 24th Ave NE
Seattle, WA 98125
USA

Telephone: (206) 362-7202

We are pleased that we could be of assistance to you and assume that you will now directly contact Mrs Smidt in the USA.

Our investigations regarding Mr Karl Stern are still in progress.

As soon as a result is known to us, we will inform you.

Till then we remain

with kind regards,

M. Schlenke

M. Schlenke
for the Archives

Grosse Allee 5 - 9, 34444 AROLSEN, Bundesrepublik Deutschland, Tel. (0 56 91) 60 37, Telegr. ITS Arolsen

We wasted no time and went to see her in July of that year. The Red Cross Society were so interested they asked if they could visit whilst we were with Dora. This newspaper article is the result.

Newspaper article of David and Dora

Red Cross reunites family torn apart by Holocaust

By Mari Herreras-Zinman
Transcript Staff

A year ago Dora Smidt would have told you the family she left behind in World War II Germany are all dead, killed in the Holocaust, but last May a phone call changed the 88-year-old's life and brought her a little hope.

Smidt, who left Germany for the Dominican Republic with her husband in 1940, says one of her older sisters left for England in 1938, and her brother, Karl, came to the states, eventually settling in Seattle, too. But her parents and other siblings all died. Last Spring, however, the American Red Cross Seattle-King County Chapter told her a nephew she never knew about has been looking for her.

" 'I am Clara's son,' he said," recalls Smidt. "I cried. The last time I saw Clara was when she left for England, and I never heard from her again. I wanted to bring her here, but no one knew where she was. We lost each other."

Now, through the Holocaust and War Victims Tracing Program, Smidt has talked and visited with Clara's son, David Stern, the first match made in Seattle by the international program. But what she discovered still upsets her.

"I can't understand that with a such a huge Jewish community that no one helped her," explains Smidt, tears lining her eyes. "It is terrible."

Stern and his wife came to Seattle last summer as part of his own personal search for his mother—eager to visit his only living relative and hoping to find information about his mother. During a telephone interview from England, Stern, who was adopted when he was eights, says he doesn't have any memories of his mother. But with help from his wife, he has placed together pieces of the mystery of what happened to Clara to England.

'This has been a bittersweet case, but this is the first time we have placed people together.'

"She hardly spoke English at all," says Stern. "I know that I was taken away from her at one point, then I was given back. Then one day, I guess she just left. She left everything behind—her purse—everything. I don't have any memory of my mother or the orphanage. I must have gone through a lot of trauma as well."

ACCORDING TO THE 55-year-old Stern, when his adopted mother died, he decided to look for Clara. His journey has taken him to his family's hometown of Gladdenbach, Germany, where he found a historian and records that showed that there were five brothers and sisters—Karl, who died in Seattle 10 years ago; Dora; Selma, who died in a concentration camp; and another uncle who died at the age of two.

David Stern and his aunt, Seattle-resident Dora Smidt, met for the first time last summer through the Holocaust and War Victims Tracing Program run by the Red Cross. This was the first reunion facilitated by the American Red Cross Seattle-King County Chapter.

"When we found Dora, I was bemused. We seemed to come to a dead end about four years ago," explains Stern, who lives with his wife in Lancaster, England. "I had lots of mixed feelings about visiting Dora. I wasn't sure if we'd all get along and what I would find out about my mother, that kind of thing."

But according to Tamara McCarthey, a Seattle Red Cross case worker who has been working with David and Dora since May, it wasn't easy finding Dora. Stern knew she married before leaving Germany, and with her brother's advice, she and her husband changed their last name from GoldSmidt to Smidt, as a precautionary measure against anti-Semitism.

From the original trace that went through the British Red Cross, McCarthey was given an old Seattle address that no longer exists. McCarthey tried to locate a new address through Department of Licensing records, but Smidt doesn't drive.

"I was ready to give up," says McCarthey. "Then as a last effort I went through the King County property tax records."

When McCarthey first contacted Smidt the Red Cross representative told her someone from England was looking for her, and Smidt hoped it was her sister, Clara. Smidt signed a release form, and on May 2 Stern and Smidt talked on the phone for only a few minutes. Then on July 7 they finally met.

"This has been a bittersweet case," says McCarthey, "but this is the first time we have placed people together."

All of this information comes through Arolsen, Germany, where the Red Cross has access to 46 million original Nazi records and documents relating to more than 14 million civilians. The center of the program, however, opened in Baltimore,

Family reunited

Continued from previous page

Md. in 1990 where 1.8 million people have discovered information on survivors. But McCarthey says it often takes a year before anyone receives information.

"I do a lot of notifications," says McCarthey, "usually about deportations, which are very difficult to tell people. It was nice to be able to see this happen from the beginning. I felt honored to be a part of it."

FOR SMIDT, THIS ends the curiosity of what happened to her sister, but it also begins a new relationship she desperately wants to have with her nephew.

Smidt holds up an old sepia-toned photograph of a young woman looking out of a window.

"When I showed this to David, it was the first time he had ever seen what his mother looks like," she says, staring at the smiling face. "I wanted her to come live with us, but everything was crazy back then."

The Lake City resident went through her own tragedy, losing her two-week old baby alone and without medical treatment in the Dominican Republic. She and her family left South America for Chicago in 1945, then later following her brother, who owned and operated a tailor shop in downtown Seattle. All along, Smidt says she worked endlessly as a seamstress in Chicago and Seattle.

According to Stern, he was overwhelmed by her family stories. The experience has changed Stern, who only recently decided to take the last name of Stern, Smidt's maiden name.

"I feel like have found my family," he says. "It is my name. I never felt close to my adopted family. I was always treated differently, but the main reason I changed my last name was in memory of my mother."

It is Dora who helped me fit the pieces together. As you can imagine, it was a bitter- sweet meeting and very emotional. Dora told me many things, but sadly could not remember everything. She must have spent a lifetime shutting out what had happened to them all. Obviously she wanted to know straightaway if we had news of Klara – sadly we didn't. She showed me many photographs and kindly lent me a couple to get copied.

David had always said, "If only I could see his mother's face." When he did, it was such a shock, in that he realised that for most of his adult life he had been looking at his mother's face, in his own daughter. It was the same face!

Picture of Klara looking through open window

Dora showed us a photograph of her on a horse in the Dominican Republic, and since then I have learned that the horse must be the one given to her and Ernst by the President. Dora didn't have many photos of past family members, but showed us what she had. She said that Karl was a weak willed man, that Getty ruled his life, and he would never do anything without her say so. As an opposite to that, Dora's eldest and youngest daughters remember him as being quite a forceful character, who held his Jewish beliefs, traditions and heritage very close to his heart. They remember very clearly an occasion when he was absolutely furious that they had a Christmas tree. He gave them a long lecture about Judaism and told Dora off for allowing it.

Karl opened a tailor's shop in downtown Seattle and according to Dora, made a lot of money during the war making officers' uniforms, and beautiful suits which were almost impossible to get hold of. He dealt in Black Market goods, especially high quality material to make men's suits. On our visit to Seattle, Getty told us he used to regularly travel by car over the Canadian border, and smuggle back to the U.S.A. vast quantities of material. It would seem that the Custom's men were often after him but never caught him, and his business went from strength to strength. Karl lived to be eighty years of age and died a fairly rich man, leaving all his wealth to Getty. He is buried in a Jewish cemetery not far from where Dora lives.

Getty, to date, is still alive, still disliked by Dora and living on the fruits of Karls labour in a very upmarket area of Seattle, known as Capitol Hill. She repeated a story about Ernst and this was it: *Sometime before Ernst died he had returned to Germany several times for a visit as he had a sister named Eulchin and a niece named Ruth who both lived in Hamburg. Sara especially remembered Eulchin as she came to visit us one year Euclhin was 4 ft. 9 inches not very tall by anyone's standards, but then most if not all my father's sisters stood between 4 ft. 9 to 5 ft. 3, the tallest man reaching 5ft. 3 inches except for one brother named Julius who died at the age of 19 from Influenza, he stood 6 foot. Anyway, Aunt Eulchin always wore a bandage on her arm and one day curiosity got the better of me and I asked her if she had cut herself, she replied that she always wore a bandage so no one would see the tattooed number on her arm. My father later told me that she had been given that number while in a Concentration Camp during the war and at some point was she had been released. We never learned which Concentration Camp she was in. Even if we had been told, we're not sure if we'd still remember. We remember her as being a rather odd duck, our father told us she was that way because she had gone through so much during the war and while she was in the camp. Her husband, we don't remember his name any longer, was just as odd, but then as the old saying goes, 'birds of a feather flock together'.*

When we returned to England, I wrote this piece for David's two children as far as my memory served me, so they would not have to wonder where they came from. I wrote it in good faith, had two copies professionally bound, and gave it to them as a Christmas present. I also wrote a very angry and subjective piece called 'Visit to Seattle' after 'Who is David?' Although what follows is a little bit repetitious, there are probably some things in it that I have forgotten to include in the body of this book.

NOVEMBER 1994 – a letter to David's children

My Dear Allison and Adrian,

This is not really a gift, more something that is yours by right. I have puzzled long and hard as to how to set down on paper, that which is your history, your heritage. The more I thought about it, the more ways I began to think of to present this to you. It became important to me that not only would it make sense and mean something to you, but also to your children and those who come after them.

In the end I have decided to write this as if I am talking to you, which in a way, I am. I shall try to be as graphic as I possibly can, incorporating all the background reading I have done, but one day I promise I will put all the finer details into a book, so that you can get a real sense of who your ancestors were, where they came from, how they lived, what trials and tribulations they had to face during their lives. The tears each one must have shed and the happiness they experienced. With luck this should help you make sense of YOURSELF, who YOU are and why you are as you are.

You are indeed very special people and I have had the good fortune to be able to get to know you over the years, initially as a child and now as a well-balanced adult. I am aware that the years have not always been kind to you. I know that your childhood and early teenage years cannot always have been completely happy. To 'lose' a dad (especially the kind your father was) must have been almost too much to cope with at times. I cannot begin to imagine what it must have been like for you when your own mum and dad split up, and then eighteen months later I came on the scene, complete with two children of my own!

I only know what I felt like at the age of seven when my own parents split up. The times in my child's mind when I fantasized that all would be well and they would 'get friends' again. Of course I was totally unaware of all the adult happenings around me and saw everything through my own eyes. As a child I had only my own sense of reason, my own knowledge of how things could/should be, my own needs and expectations that at the time, were not being fulfilled. I learned to make sense of this in the only way I knew how and as a consequence I learned to survive, as you did, as your Dad did and as all those who went before him; but I often wonder what all this does to us as people. Does it make us better or worse? I have no answers to this.

It seems that as we get older we lose many valuable, magic ways of looking at things but in return we gain wisdom and acceptance. Our priorities change and we begin to mellow. Different things make us happy and hurt us; some things take on a greater importance and others pale into insignificance. However, I do believe that the need to love and be loved and to belong stays with us for always.

So that you can follow the story of your ancestors, I will start at the beginning. That is to say as far as I, and others who have helped me to trace the Family Stern back to the 1700's. In between trying to explain what has been discovered factually, I have assumed a lot.

Wolf (your 4 times great-grandfather), seems to have been an intelligent and interesting man who tried his best to live by the laws and traditions of Judaism and all that goes with it. It seems that in his early twenties he was quite well known, powerful and influential. He seemed to live his life fighting for those less able than himself and when he died, he was quite a rich man. He died when he was quite old, even by today's standards – old age seems to run in your family.

Although Wolf acquired land and money, life was not easy for him, especially when he changed his name to a Christian name. He was surrounded by prejudice and change. He seemed to have made an effort to speak 'High German' but it could have been with a Yiddish accent. To Wolf a good education for all his children was everything. Even though the Rabbis were very powerful (they still are) Wolf did not mind the influence they had on his children. He seems to have made a good living from money lending and strangely enough Jews are to this day, still at the heart of businesses involving the lending of money. Just think about the families Goldsmith and Rothschild.

As you know, Jews did not marry until at least their late twenties and onwards, past forty sometimes, and they had to obtain permission to do this. Wolfe could be considered to be getting on when his youngest son Abraham was born. I do not know anything about Abraham's childhood or his relationship with his parents.

It is an exceptional fact that by the time Abraham was grown up he was allowed to join the Army and he did. I don't know if his parents supported that decision or not. Nevertheless he proved to be a good soldier. His parents must have thought they would never see him again. He was away for six years and had no contact with them. How they coped is anybody's guess. My own grandfathers were away from home for four years and needed to re-establish their relationships with their wives and children on return. Four years is a long time, six is even longer and the horrors of any war are too difficult to contemplate.

Soon after he left the Army he changed his name to Christian Reinhardt after his Christian Godfather and converted to Christianity. He returned to live in Gladenbach in 1823 at the age of 34. He married soon after for the first time and it seems he became a peddler or 'schnorrer' because there was nothing else for him to do. Maybe he had an argument with his father and was unable to go into the family business. He divorced his wife after a few years and married again after he had converted back to Judaism. When he was 41 he was a rich man, it is recorded that he had 8,000 Guilders that in this day and age would be worth roughly about half a million pounds! He married again after only two years, she died after eight years. Maybe she died of some disease that was rife at the time. Abraham lived until he was quite old.

Simon, who was Abraham's son, was born in 1833 and did not get married until he was 41, true to form for Jews then. I do not know anything about his childhood or his time as a young man. He married a girl from the next village whose father was an established butcher. Maybe as part of the wedding dowry Simon was made a partner in the butchers shop. It would not be unusual for this to happen. Prior to this he is recorded as being a second-hand dealer and the woman he married was one also. What they dealt it is anyone's guess.

The night I met your dad (way back in 1973), some of the first things he said to me were about identity and belonging. He introduced himself as David, a Jew, who didn't know where he was from, who his people were or where he was going. In essence, he didn't have a sense of himself. He was keen for me to know that he was alone but he had two children whom he loved dearly. They were, in fact, as far as he was concerned, his only family, his only heritage. They were the only things in his life that mattered.

This has been an eventful year and you know the results, but later on I will spell it out for the benefit of others who may one day read this. Maybe others who one day read this will then begin not only to get a sense of the past, but also a sense of who we all are/were, and why it seemed so important in November 1994 to set it all down on paper. Along with the photographs, it should provide a reasonable picture.

It seems a little strange that I am writing this in order to present it to you, along with a collection of family photographs; for Christmas when your real heritage is Jewish. Maybe I should be timing this gift for Chanukah- The Jewish Festival of Light celebrated in December. After all, this is intended to bring light into your life and Chanukah is a time for giving gifts.

There was one particular time when we were in the South of England and dad decided that he wanted to visit Tunbridge Wells. This was the place he remembered being in a children's home, this was the place he was adopted from. This and three other memories were all he had to go on. One memory consisted of being in the children's home and being punished for doing something naughty, he was made to climb a ladder into a dark loft, the hatch was then closed and the ladder taken away. He was left there for what he remembers, was a long time. He felt very frightened and alone. He must have been around seven years old at the time.

Another one was of someone picking him up, he was much smaller then, and running through the streets to the sounds of wartime sirens, seeking the safety of the air-raid shelters. The third and most important memory as far as he is concerned, was that of his real name. Dad always knew he was called David Stern.

Dad tried desperately to remember what the children's home looked like and where it was but couldn't find it. His only memory was that of an old house with a clock tower. He decided to ask his adoptive mother for the correct address. She was extremely put out and said she couldn't remember it or where it was, so that was the end of that! Dad didn't want to hurt her so he buried the longing for a few more years.

When your dad's adoptive mother died, I encouraged your him to apply for his original Birth Certificate and in October 1984 he obtained a copy. We told your adoptive grandfather what we were doing and he suddenly produced some original letters from the children's home your Dad was in, also some other letters from the Charity that had dealt with your dad and his mother. I contacted lots of addresses, we visited London and found the place he was born, and on his fiftieth birthday I took him on a surprise visit to Gladenbach. This was the village where his mother was born, as you know.

One person in particular (Jurgen Rundshiemer) has been a key figure in piecing together the history. I have him to thank for so many things. We are still in touch six years later and he is still uncovering valuable information. I think it is important that you know he is not Jewish. He is a kind, gentle man, with so much insight into the needs of those who want to trace relatives. I understand he was the Headmaster of the local school before he retired. Since retirement, he has made it almost his life's work to gather together what happened to all the Jews from Gladenbach. He is a very clever archivist and so dedicated. I know that we are not the only people he has helped and is helping. During that first visit he was able to tell us so much we did not know. Real and concrete information that Klara had a brother, and two sisters and the names of her parents.

I will insert copies of the relevant and interesting documents I have unearthed. Perhaps one day you will be able to add to these and keep the story going.

Up until the summer of this year, I didn't know much more about your great-grandparents, other than the fact that they were listed as the last remaining Jews in Gladenbach in October 1939, and where and when they died, but during the ten years I have spent researching the family, I had learned a lot about Klara. To help you piece this part of the history together I need to go back to when I started the search.

As I said at the beginning, the first real evidence we had was your dad's original birth certificate and also the letters David's adoptive father suddenly produced. From there on it was a question of following every possible lead.

Each year a little more information came to light, copies of important documents were found and I was able to piece the story together, building up a fairly clear picture of Klara after she arrived in England, but only so far! (I have included all the documents and papers that I think you will find interesting in this book.)

Always there were pieces of the jigsaw missing. There still are but not so many! I always believed that someone of the Stern family would still be alive and would have some pieces to fit the jigsaw. By 1992 I had exhausted every avenue and finally put the search in the hands of the International Red Cross.

In June of that year, a letter arrived telling us that Dora, (Adolph and Sarah's youngest daughter who is now 83) was alive and well and living in Seattle, U.S.A. As you know we wasted no time and went to see her in July. It is 'Dora' who has helped me fit the final pieces together.

Dora first of all, was able to confirm how well respected and loved Adolph and Sarah were and how kind they were to others less fortunate than themselves. She remembers her childhood as very happy and carefree. Jewish traditions, festivals and dietary laws were observed and the family regularly attended 'schul'. The house on Burgstrasse was still their home and they were quite financially comfortable. The girls were trained in all 'household' duties and also as seamstresses. Karl was trained as a tailor. Apparently Selma was 'the clever one'. The girls used to go walking in the local parkland and meet young men (always Jewish!) They kept this secret from their father, as he would have frowned upon such behaviour. Then along came Hitler and his followers early in the 1930's. By this time, Selma, Karl, Klara and Dora were in their twenties.

Once again, as Jews, they were under threat. By 1933 Hitler had managed to convince many people with his ideas and Jewish people were amongst the first to suffer (Dora was quick to point out that many other non-Jewish people suffered too!) From all the material I have read it seems it was not that difficult for Hitler to convince people. All the old prejudices were still there (even if under the surface) and it didn't help that, generally speaking, the Jews were successful in business, were better off than many others and had quite a lot of power, especially in the economy of Germany. The German people were trapped in a deep financial depression. Many people were starving; it was almost impossible even to buy a loaf of bread! Unemployment was high, social problems were rife. At the time Hitler came along, people were looking for a 'saviour'. In the early years he 'proved' himself to the people by putting people to work, building roads and railways and generally improving the lot of many individuals.

I don't especially want to recount all the happenings there were in the years leading up to and during the War between 1939 - 1945. They must have been terrible times to live in, and I think history speaks for itself.

Dora looked after her mother for several months, until she was well again. Dora never returned to Frankfurt as some elderly, rich friends of Adolph and Sarah asked Dora if she would go and be their housekeeper and look after them. Dora agreed and went to live in a place that was so awful it cannot be described. Dora was able to tell me several stories that support my feelings and beliefs. She remembers soldiers and young people marching through the streets of Gladenbach singing songs in support of Hitler, his beliefs and the notion of a 'perfect' Fatherland. Life in the village became more and more difficult and in 1935 Adolph and Sarah encouraged the three sisters, Selma, Klara and Dora, to leave the village and move to Frankfurt until everything calmed down and returned to normal, in the belief that it would be easier for them to keep a low profile in a large city where they were not known. Many thousands of Jews did exactly the same thing. Adolph firmly believed that he was witnessing yet another bout of anti-semitism that would soon die down, after all, he and his ancestors before him were no strangers to it. The 'familiar' held no fears for him. How could he have even suspected things would turn out as they did? Dora cannot remember what their brother Karl did at this time.

Somewhere around this time, Adolph's best friend (Adolph, who had fought in the first world war with him), wrote to your great grandfather begging him and his family, to leave Germany. He had, two years before, emigrated to America and was doing well. From the outside looking in, he could obviously see the writing on the wall. He even offered to pay all their travels costs (by this time, Jews were only allowed to take a very small amount of money out of the country and had to leave all their property, houses etc. behind). He also offered to provide them with a house in America. Great grandfather Adolph was very stubborn, he refused to believe he, or his wife, were in danger. He also refused point blank to leave his birthplace and his home, saying he was too old for change.

The three sisters stayed close in those early days in Frankfurt. Selma had a job working for a doctor (I think as a receptionist), Klara became a housekeeper for a rich Jewish family and Dora worked at the local hospital making nurses uniforms. They used to meet regularly at weekends and go out together. Life must have been very different for them after the cosiness of the village, especially in a climate of growing hatred of the Jews.

About a year later (Dora's memory is not very clear on times and dates), Sarah's mother was ill and needed nursing back to health. It was Dora who returned to Gladenbach to undertake this task. She stayed with her mother until she was well, and then moved to a place called Altenkirchen, to look after an elderly couple who were friends of Dora's parents. It was here that she met her husband Ernst Goldschmidt.

From here on I will tell you the stories of each individual and what happened to them as far as I can. Adolph and Sarah stayed on in Gladenbach right up until June 1940. By then Germany had been at war for ten months and many

Jews along with many others, had been incarcerated in concentration camps and died there. I have been unable to find out if they left Gladenbach of their own free will or if they were arrested there, transported to Frankfurt and then on to a camp. The records show they left the village together on 17.06.1940. The documents from the Red Cross do not show the date of their arrest, only the date they arrived at the concentration camp 'Ghetto Theresienstadt'. This was the 16th September 1942. I have since discovered that this particular camp was known as a transitional camp. From there, prisoners were either moved on to the 'death camps' of Auschwitz, Buchenwald etc or, they died there. It is quite possible they were in another camp between June 1940 and September 1942.

Sarah survived only six weeks after her arrival at Theresienstadt, her date of death was 2nd November 1942. Adolph survived longer and died on 4th December 1943. They were both 69 when they died. What horrors they were subjected to and witnessed, and exactly how they died no-one will ever know as those details were not included on their Death Certificates.

What happened to Selma (your Great Aunt) in the years between her arrival in Frankfurt and her death is not really known at the moment. Dora lost touch with her after she moved to Altenkirchen. It looks like Selma stayed on in Frankfurt as her last known address, before arrest, is listed as 'Grunstrasse 42'. She was evacuated to the East, (many of the camps were in the East, well away from preying eyes) on September 24th 1942 by the Geheime Staatspolzei. The pictures in my mind conjure up those horrific scenes of thousands of Jews herded into cattle trucks and transported by railway to the death camps.

Selma must have spent some time in one camp before finally being committed to Concentration Camp Stutthof by the Sicherheitpolizei Riga on the 23rd August 1944. Amongst other things, she may have suffered the indignity of being stripped naked of all her possessions and clothing, had her head shaved and a number tattooed on her arm. Her prisoner number was 70550. Selma died on 21st December 1944 aged 42 having never married. The reason recorded is 'cardiac weakness'. I suspect she ended her life in the gas chambers, as this was often the reason given for this kind of death.

Dora is not very clear about where Karl lived during these times or, what he did. She can only say that in the year (1938) leading up to the outbreak of war, Jews were encouraged to leave Germany, never to return. There were, however, lots of conditions. By this time they were allowed to take only 40 Kilos of luggage and ten marks. I'm not sure what this was worth then but I think it was a mere pittance! All Dora knows is that he got out of Germany and arrived in America via Russia and China. I could imagine his journey would have been pretty hair-raising! The rule was that you could leave Germany and enter a new country if you had a sponsor in the country you were aiming for. Karl must have had a contact in America. Maybe it was his father's best friend, Adolph. Both Dora and Klara must have known where he was heading as they wrote letters to each other.

Karl chose Seattle as the place to live and very quickly established himself as a tailor and dry-cleaner. (At this point in time he would have been around the age of 37). Soon after he settled there, he married a German-Jewish refugee called Getty (correct name Gertrude I think). She already had one child and was pregnant at the time of the marriage. Dora says that the pregnancy (who turned out to be her son Stan who we met on our visit) was nothing to do with Karl. She is adamant that Stan was not Karl's son, although he bears the name Stern.

Karl opened a tailor's shop in downtown Seattle and according to Dora, made a lot of money during the war making officers' uniforms and beautiful suits that were almost impossible to get hold of. He dealt in Black Market goods, especially high quality material to make men's suits. On our visit to Seattle, Getty told us he used to regularly travel by car, over the Canadian border and smuggle back to the U.S.A. vast quantities of material. A totally illegal pursuit! It would seem that the Customs Men were often after him, but never caught him, and his business went from strength to strength.

Getty was, and still is, a very strong character. Dora says that Karl was a weak willed man and Getty ruled his life. He would never do anything without her say so. She was very possessive and extremely caught up with the need for money and status. She's still the same! As an opposite to that, Dora's daughter's, remember him as being quite a forceful character who held his Jewish beliefs, traditions and heritage very close to his heart. They remember very clearly an occasion when he was absolutely furious that they had a Christmas tree. He gave them a long lecture about Judaism and told Dora off for allowing it.

Karl lived to be eighty years of age and died a fairly rich man leaving all his wealth to Getty. He is buried in a Jewish cemetery not far from where Dora lives. Getty, to date, is still alive and living on the fruits of his labour in a very 'upmarket' area of Seattle known as Capitol Hill. She is quite old now and not a particularly well woman. Stan told me he is waiting for her to die so that he can spend all the money travelling the world!

What of Klara? This part of the story is the most painful for me to write and probably for you to read. Klara was your grandmother, but more important than that, your dad's mother! I have learned, thought, read and discussed with Dora, so much about her, that to me she is a very real person. I feel like I knew her and yet I never did. Dora's recollections of their childhood and the early days in Frankfurt are of a sweet, gentle, loving older sister who was always laughing. They were so close it is impossible to describe. Dora loved her very much. As did everyone else she came into contact with, it seems she was always ready to help someone and was a real 'giver'.

Klara was very pretty, with beautiful dark hair and hazel eyes. When Dora described her to me it was like someone describing your Dad. Klara also stayed on in Frankfurt after Dora went back to Gladenbach to care for their mother. Whilst Dora was away, (this is a story Dora told me), Klara had a very deep and intense love affair. He was married (a total sin in Jewish law and tradition) and eventually he left her and disappeared. Nobody knows why, but the result was that Klara was so distressed that she threw herself from an upstairs window. She must have been badly hurt as both her parents and Dora were notified. Great grandad Adolph apparently blamed Dora, as she had been the one who had introduced them! Dora wrote to Klara asking her 'why had she done such a thing?' Klara had replied that she loved him so much; nothing else had any meaning anymore.

Klara must have recovered enough to survive, as it wasn't until the end of 1938 that she escaped from Germany. She didn't actually leave until the end of December that year, so she must have witnessed some terrible things happening around her, if not to her. The night of the 9/10th of November of that year was the notorious 'Kristallnacht', (the night of the broken glass). On that night a co-ordinated attack on all the known Jews in Germany was launched. Gangs of Brown Shirts and civilians roamed the streets, destroying by smashing windows, furniture, belongings, stock, treasured possessions, all Jewish shops, houses, businesses and synagogues. They smashed everything in sight that had any hint of Judaism. Thousands of Jewish men were beaten up and arrested on that night and transported to concentration camps. Many of them never returned to their homes and families.

Prior to this terrible night, Klara must have met either someone else she thought she loved, or her lover returned, as when she left Germany she was slightly more than five months pregnant. Working back from your dad's birthday, she must have conceived him in late July of 1938. The awful thing is, your dad's father (your grandad) may have been one of the men arrested, never to return, on that awful night. That bit of the jigsaw we will never know! Whatever happened I have no doubt that Klara was completely distraught to find herself pregnant and alone in such circumstances.

By then, Jews were being made to wear the Yellow Star to identify them as Jews and therefore were the enemies of the state of Germany. It was becoming more and more difficult to get out of the country and more and more Jews were disappearing, never to be seen again. At the same time, other countries were beginning to close their doors to Jews. It was now almost impossible to emigrate, even though Hitler wanted to get rid of Jews any way he could. The more strongly Jews felt the pressure to leave Germany, the more reluctant became the potential countries of refuge to accept them. Britain introduced a visa system in order to achieve a better control of the influx of refugees, but lifted the restrictions for certain categories such as trans-migrants, domestics, children and those refugees whose maintenance was guaranteed.

Klara entered Britain on a Domestics Visa, but maybe she was also able to say that she was only intending to stay a short while as she had people in the U.S.A. who would vouch for her and that was where she was eventually intending to go. Even on a domestics visa she would have had to have a sponsor. Perhaps friends of hers or the family had come before her.

The history books tell me that life was very difficult for refugees in Britain then. Following 'Kristallnacht', the rest of November and December 1938, saw thousands of children and adults arrive in England, by boat, via Harwich. This was where Klara arrived on New Year's Eve (31st December) 1938. Sponsors often did not want to know the people whom they had sponsored once they arrived, and many of the refugees were forced to register with new charities that had been hastily set up to deal with them. So many charities, all bearing different names were set up all over the country.

All were registered and had representatives at a place in London called 'Bloomsbury House'. When you turn these pages and read Klara's case notes, you will see many references to B.H., that is Bloomsbury House, and it is still there.

Children, or adults who entered on a domestics visa represented the majority of refugees who entered Britain at this time. Although there were some Christian organisations who acted as sponsors, most of the refugees had to rely on their own people i.e. either friends from Germany or, more commonly, on relatives who had emigrated before them. Most of the refugees lived in awful conditions in bed-sitters, (Klara changed addresses many times) far away from anyone they knew, and where they were not really wanted. Anti-Semitism was also fairly rife and of course everybody in England hated the Germans. After all, they were at war with them!

The German-Jewish Aid Committee published a brochure entitled:

'While you are in England: Helpful Information and Guidance for every Refugee.'

It contained eight commandments to teach refugees good behaviour so as not to provoke any animosity. Refugees were asked to: - "Refrain from speaking German in the streets and in public conveyances and in public places such as restaurants. Talk halting English rather than fluent German. Do not criticize any Government regulations, nor the way things are done over here. Do not speak of 'how much better this or that is done in Germany.'"

'It may be true in some matters, but it weighs as nothing against the sympathy and freedom and liberty of England, which are now given to you. Never forget that point....Do not make yourself conspicuous by speaking loudly, nor by your manner of dress....The Englishman attaches very great importance to modesty, under-statement in speech rather than over-statement, and quietness of dress and manner. He values good manners far more than he values evidence of wealth....Do not spread the poison of "It's bound to come in your country." The British Jew greatly objects to the planting of this craven thought... Above all, please realise that the Jewish Community is relying on you - each and every-one of you - to uphold in this country the highest Jewish qualities, to maintain dignity, and to help serve others.'

What it must have been like for Klara, in this climate, to have nothing except the knowledge of the horrors that were happening in her homeland, to come from a fairly middle-class family and be expected to be a domestic servant, to be completely alone and know no-one, to speak no English and be on the receiving end of negative attitudes and prejudice, to be five months pregnant, to not know what had happened to her family and maybe, her lover, or if she would ever see them again, is beyond my comprehension. I will leave you to read the case notes and draw your own conclusions.

I feel sure that when you have read all those 'notes', you will be more clear as to what life was like for your grandmother as a refugee in England, and I think, as it did for me, will have raised many questions for you. You can see that for much of the time, she was subject to being moved around at other people's whim.

She was obviously not particularly physically fit after she had your dad, and had to rely on whatever medical attention and emotional support that was selected and given to her. One book I have read called 'German-Jewish Refugees in England', by Marion Berghahn, tells of the difficulties and traumas faced by people like your grandmother. The rate of mental illness and suicide was unbelievably high amongst this group of people. It's not surprising when you think of all they had been through, and all they had left behind! Putting all the pieces together I think Klara probably was suffering from post-natal depression, and nobody realised this.

I do know she wrote letters to Karl in America, and tried desperately to contact Dora by advertising in a well known German-Jewish newspaper called Aufbau. Just for the record, when I advertised in Aufbau in 1989 to see if I could find anyone - there was no positive result!

The reason I am able to tell you about Klara's search for Karl and Dora is that, during our stay with her, she told me several stories relating to Klara. She had only found out the truth, years later and is very bitter about this.

Klara must have had an address for Karl in America as she wrote to him several times, begging him to send her a ticket to America. It seems that Getty did not want Klara invading their marriage, and she certainly didn't want to share their newfound wealth. She convinced Karl that Klara was mentally ill. If you add this on top of Karl's Jewish prejudice, i.e. anyone who indulged in sex before marriage was disgusting, you can begin to see why he would not respond. He said he was ashamed of Klara having a baby outside of marriage; this fact convinced him that she did not deserve help. As far as he was concerned, she was no longer a member of his family. She was a non-person. What this kind of response must have done to Klara, I don't know. I believe she must have felt totally abandoned.

As far as Klara's advertisement looking for Dora is concerned, apparently Karl saw it and Dora didn't. He never told her but kept it for years. It was only about ten years before he died that he told Dora. He was very nasty about it and tore the advert up in front of her. Dora has never come to terms with this and spent many hours talking about it to us. She kept saying, "If only I had known, I would have sent for my sister and her child and looked after them, but he never told me!" As a consequence she has a lot of negative feelings towards Karl and Getty. Who can blame her! Sadly she also carries a lot of guilt.

As you know, the war ended in 1945, but for quite some time afterwards, England was still in a state of flux. I don't know if Klara continued to try to leave the country and build a new life for herself and David, but from the notes it seems that she was a very sad woman, under pressure to give up her rights to her child, living from day to day wherever she could, without any real financial support, and trying to do her best in the most awful of circumstances.

On April 24th 1946, she walked out of the hostel she was living in, never to be seen again. All her belongings were left behind. My intuition tells me she that she felt so alone and desolate that she had finally come to a point where she could no longer cope and carry on.

I believe it is quite possible that, having lost everything and everybody she cared about, (including her child), she made that final step into the unknown and took her own life. Perhaps she even made sure there was nothing on her person to identify her. What had she to live for?

Why there was a delay of four months in launching a search for her I cannot understand. Once a search was made, it seems it was too late. Klara had disappeared without trace. All the searches and checks of records made over the years (including my own) have turned up nothing. This, I believe, will always be another one of the pieces of the jigsaw that will never be found. The saddest part of the story, Klara was the most important link.

To me, it feels like nobody was particularly bothered about her disappearance except for the fact that your dad had, at this point, joined the thousands of other refugee children in need of a long-term home and someone, or some agency would have to attend to this need.

And so to Dora. Hers, in a way, is a happier story, although her life has been filled with much sadness and many tragedies. As I said earlier on, she went from Frankfurt back home to Gladenbach, and then on to a place called Altenkirchen to care for an elderly Jewish couple. It was here that she met Ernst Goldschmidt. He was studying for a Ph.D. in Agriculture (he already had a good Degree) and was living in lodgings across the street. According to Dora he was very handsome, not at all Jewish looking, as he had blonde hair and blue eyes. He courted her and they fell in love. Although this was well before 1939 (the outbreak of war), life was very difficult for all and especially for Jews.

Hitler had come to power in 1933 and by this time men were being forced to work on so called 'projects' to put Germany back on its feet. Thousands of men, Christians as well as Jews, were sent away from home to work on new road and railway systems, clearing the land as they went, all over Germany and especially in the East. These men had to work up to twelve, sometimes fourteen hours a day for a mere pittance. Ernst was one of these men. However, the people thought it was better than not working at all and there were unconfirmed rumours that if you didn't obey, you were sent to a 'camp' and possibly tortured. One of the better-known propaganda slogans was 'bread for all!' (Women were also made to work in factories for long hours and little pay).

He was sent away to a remote part of Germany on the Polish border, to work on a new railway. At this point no one knew he was Jewish. Whenever he could, he kept in touch with Dora by letter, and messages via friends of friends.

Time went by and Dora continued to care for the elderly couple and devote some time to her own little sewing business. All the while Anti-Semitism was growing, and there were more and more incidents of Jews being beaten up, hounded, ostracized, arrested on false charges and sent to concentration camps. Hitler had convinced the people that Jews needed 'educating to work' as they were lazy and therefore enemies of the State, by 'concentrating' them in camps, they could be educated and made into useful citizens.

Groups of soldiers and brown shirts intimidating Jews, singing Anti-Semitic songs and shouting Sieg Heil! Hiel Hitler! through the streets and into the night; raping Jewish women and generally terrorising the Jewish population became the norm. Dora has many vivid memories of this time. One very clear memory that has stayed with her and probably will until the day she dies, is of the night when three young Gestapo Officers hammered on the door of the house where she lived with the elderly couple. Dora was upstairs and the owners were downstairs. For quite some time they pretended that no one was in, they were so terrified.

Eventually, the elderly man realised he would have to open the door or the soldiers would break it down. Dora remembers hearing the front door being opened, raised, harsh voices and then the sound of screaming. She rushed out of her room and stood at the top of the stairs, there to witness the most horrendous scene she had ever seen in her life. The three young soldiers were systematically beating the elderly couple in the hallway. Dora recalls that she was trembling with rage and shouted at the top of her voice for them to stop whilst she was descending the flight of stairs.

She finally reached the bottom and demanded to know why they were doing this, she confronted one of the soldiers, (who she said was younger than her), looked into his eyes and said "Why, why do you do this, they are old, would you do this to your grandparents?"

Something she said must have touched a nerve in the young soldier as he looked at the others and seemed to pass a silent message to them. As one, all three, stopped what they were doing and silently left the house, banging the door behind them.

It was only later that Dora began to realise that she had taken her life in her hands in standing up to these men. She could so easily have been beaten also or even arrested and transported to a camp. She still, to this day, cannot understand why the soldiers left her alone.

Late on in 1938, Ernst was still working as a slave on the railway. The pressure to expose Jews was by now enormous. How it came about I do not know, but one day someone reported the fact that he was a Jew to the Gestapo. The foreman of the work gang liked Ernst very much and tipped him off. The Foreman told the Gestapo that Ernst was sick and would not be in to work for a few days, and that he didn't know his address. This gave Ernst some precious time to escape. He headed for Altenkirchen, to Dora. He asked her to marry him and escape from Germany with him. Dora agreed and they left for Gelsenkirchen, the place where Ernst was born and where his family were. Ernst came from a big family, and had fourteen brothers and sisters.

They were married there, I think so much in haste that it was impossible to inform Dora's family.

Only a few days afterwards, Ernst managed to secure a job that offered the opportunity to leave Germany. He was to work for the President of the Dominican Republic, teaching the people how to cultivate the land. (In case you don't know, the Dominican Republic is the other half of the tropical island of Haiti, situated in the Caribbean, almost next door to Cuba, off the coast of Florida.)

They left Gelsenkirchen (Dora remembers everyone waving them off at the railway station) and headed for the coast of Germany where they boarded an Italian boat, along with twenty-four others who were also contracted to do similar work, to set sail for this foreign land.

I find it difficult to imagine what king of a journey this was. Dodging the Gestapo, only to be faced with what probably turned out to be a nightmare of a journey that must have lasted weeks.

In the late thirties, the Dominican Republic would have been extremely under-developed. Most of the land was covered in Tropical forests. Although they were now no longer in fear of their lives from the Gestapo, they had unsanitary conditions, disease, horrible biting insects and snakes and unrelenting heat and humidity to contend with. Whilst Ernst worked the land, Dora had to care for eight of the single men who had arrived with them. She worked from morning till night, washing, cooking and keeping the house clean as best she could. Nearly all of the landed refugees suffered from malaria and medical attention was impossible to obtain. Their only rewards being a place to live and a meagre salary.

Not long after their arrival, Dora became pregnant. She told me she had a very difficult pregnancy and was ill for most of the time. When she finally went into labour, no doctor or midwife could be found for many miles around. Her baby was delivered with great difficulty, and in the most unhygienic circumstances you can imagine. Even amongst all this she and Ernst were ecstatic that they now had a son, their firstborn. Tragically the baby died within only a few short days. Dora says neither of them ever really came to terms with this. They both continued to labour on in this disease-ridden island for the next five years.

In 1944, their daughter Sarah was born. Before she was one year old, Sarah had also contracted Malaria and Dora thought she might lose her too. In 1945, they decided enough was enough, they could no longer cope with the enforced lifestyle they lived, and decided that even though they had little money, they would leave the Dominican Republic and head for America.

Initially they went by boat from the island to Florida, and from there to Chicago, where one of Ernst's sisters had settled. She had a small Kosher restaurant there. On arrival, they changed their surname to Smidt to avoid any prejudice. (Another name change!) Ernst soon learned that only six of his brothers and sisters had escaped the Holocaust. All the rest had been arrested and sent to camps.

For six months they lived with Ernst's sister but Dora was very unhappy. She constantly felt in the way, and did not feel at all welcome. It was also wintertime and neither of them were used to the bitter Chicago weather.

Karl encouraged them to move to Seattle where by now, he was fast becoming a well-established businessman. Dora believed Karl would help them out when they got there but that was not to be. Karl professed to be glad to see them but did not offer either shelter or any financial help. They rented a tiny flat and turned their energies to finding work. Poor Ernst was never to work on the land again. The only work he could find was in a bakery. He stayed in this job literally until the day he died.

In the beginning, Dora took in sewing work at home whilst Sarah was small, another child, Mona, was born in 1948. Later Dora found a job in a sweat shop and worked all the hours she could make men's neckties for a few cents each. She would then go home, attend to her family and then continue to sew and repair items people had brought her until late into the night.

Gradually their financial situation improved and they moved first to a bigger rented apartment, then a rented house and finally they bought the house where she still lives. One bitter memory Dora has is of when she was caught out in the pouring rain on a freezing cold day, with Sarah who was a toddler at the time. She only had a few cents to her name, but decided to catch a bus home to save the child from the long walk in such awful weather. She was feeling very down as she was wondering where the next meal was coming from, but her heart lifted when she spotted Karl on the bus. She hoped he would notice how hard-up she was and offer help. Karl chose to ignore her by turning his back, pretending not to see her. The hurt of that day has stayed with her all these years.

From there on, Dora and Ernst made the best of their lives, always looking ahead, never backwards. They gave their two daughters everything that is humanly possible for two parents to give. This of course, included lots of love. In a way, maybe they gave them too much, as both Dora's girls are now grown up but behave like two, very spoiled children. They are all, in fact, a very dysfunctional family. Sarah lives next door to Dora, and her sister only lives a couple of miles away, but Dora gets little help from them. Neither of them seem to appreciate or understand the hard times and traumas their parents went through. Perhaps Dora and Ernst (who died six years ago), have to take some responsibility for this. Dora admits they sheltered the girls from all the horrors, and only ever told them happy stories of their own childhood and early adulthood in Germany, never about the Nazis or the terrible times.

The fact that Dora is now eighty-three, alone and needs affection, practical help and support and doesn't really get any of these things from her daughters is a bitter pill for your dad to swallow. He would give anything to have a mother to care for and surround with love. His unfulfilled wish in life was to have been a kind and loving son. Life is very cruel isn't it! Having now found Dora he lives in fear of losing her. She is so far away and time is so short. I think the weekly telephone calls he makes to her only add to his frustration.

This really only leaves me now with the story of David, your dad, as it will be up to you to record the happenings in your life for the benefit of your children and your children's children. I have already told you of the few scant memories he has of his early years. He must have been through so much that his mind has completely blanked out any memories of his mother and the times they were together. The 'notes' show how he was taken from her and moved around to foster-parents, residential nurseries and children's homes. Usually a long way from where Klara was, which must have made it so difficult for her to visit him regularly, although she obviously did her best for him.

The records show that he was interned with her on the Isle of Man (which became known as the Island of Barbed Wire). In spite of being 'interned' I can imagine that these were some of the happiest days for them both. That time together must have been very precious. After their release and return to mainland England, it seems clear that once again he was taken from Klara. Within a year of her disappearance (he was eight years old by then), he was placed with the people you came to know as your grandparents, David's adoptive father and mother They already had two children, a boy aged ten and a girl aged four.

He lived with them from then on and in 1950, without Klara being presumed dead, they legally adopted him and changed his name from Stern to theirs. They were financially very comfortable, and gave your dad everything - except love and affection! He was always made to feel different and somehow had a sense of having to feel grateful for what they did for him. This fact was re-affirmed when his adoptive father and mother both died within three years of each other. David's adoptive mother left him nothing, not even a little keepsake, and his adoptive father named David as 'my adopted son' in his Will, and left him five thousand pounds.

The rest of the estate, some £100,000 was left to his 'real' children.

Between the ages of eight and sixteen, when he went away to Catering College, his memories are neither happy nor sad, he was only conscious of being different and alone. I often get the feeling they were the 'wilderness years'.

After College, your dad never really returned home to the West-Samuel household. As you know, after a relatively short courtship, he married your mother. With hindsight he now knows he used the fact that she was pregnant as an escape route. To get married and create a family of his own might fill the gaps in his life. He would no longer feel or be alone. The greatest joy in his life was when his children were born. Now he had a family, people to call his own. He has always loved you dearly; you were and are, his roots and his anchor. Even though he now knows who he is and where he came from, no one will ever replace the special place you fill in his heart and soul.

It was almost more than he could bear when his marriage to your mother fell apart and he was unable to be with you every day. The night I met him, which was eighteen months after they had separated, he was a sad and lonely man. What has happened in the years between then and now you know. I know I don't need to describe him to you, but it feels important to me that those who read this in later years are able to get a real sense of him. I am not sure what I can say about him except that he is a good, kind, strong and sensitive man. He is one of life's true 'givers' who never really asks for anything in return, and I love him dearly. He is warm and affectionate and he has a lovely sense of humour. He has the kindest eyes I have ever seen.

He is very handsome and also proud to be a Jew. We have been together now for 21 years and this month he has finally reclaimed his identity - he has legally changed his name back to Stern! I told you changing names appears to be a recurrent theme in your family. It was very important to Dad as he sees himself as the last of the Stern family to bear the name. From now on he will proudly carry the name his mother gave him. As his wife, I have also changed my name. I think Christina Stern sounds quite impressive and I shall be happy to be known by this name.

We first met in January 1973. At that time we had both experienced a broken marriage and were very unhappy. We got married in 1977. Throughout these years he has been a wonderful husband, friend and cornerstone to me. He has tried his very best to be a good father to you, sometimes against difficult odds and maybe not always successfully. When Louis and Sophie were born, his joy was complete. The pleasure he gets from being a grandfather is indescribable. His most precious moments are those spent with the little ones. In return they love him too!

Dad has spent all his adult life in the Hotel and Catering Industry and he has many qualifications in this subject. He has managed large hotels and restaurants, had his own Pubs and has also worked on the wholesale side, selling meat to Hotels and Restaurants. Always he has worked very hard for very little in return. Now he has his own place about ten miles from where we live. It is a cafe called 'The Big Breakfast' and serves traditional English breakfasts all day! He enjoys it very much and can turn his hand to anything. He is a very good cook! After us, his family, and the business, his other loves in life are flying (yes, he really does love to fly a plane, and at the age of fifty studied for his

Private Pilot's Licence, I was very proud of him), and also gardening.

We live in a tiny cottage that dates back to 1638 (it was built more than a hundred years before this story starts!) just cosy for the two of us. The house has a large, typically English cottage garden where we spend many happy hours together, and it is our pride and joy. Where we live is in the countryside surrounded by farms. Just a little bit like Gladenbach. 'Family days', when you and all the rest of our lovely family come to see us, are very important to us both and a source of great delight. We enjoy those happy family meals and treasure the good times together. But until recently, however good those times were, there was always something missing for dad - his own family roots, a sense of the past, his heritage, his history!

In short, 'David's People.'

You now know as much as I do. It is up to you to build upon it, and extend it in the future, so that your descendants never have to ponder the questions, "Who am I?", and, "Where did I come from?" The pleasure and reward for me is to be able to pass on to you that which is yours, by right.

This is for Klara - who I never knew and for David - who I know so well!

May 2003 saw me working at the University and as well as teaching, placing students for a practical experience. One student begged me for a placement in the Isle of Man. Ridiculous that I had never been, when it is only 80 miles off the mainland and we live about 5 minutes away from the port. Anyway, I had to check out the placement and thought I would kill two birds with one stone and contact by email the Librarian Archivist there in. He emailed me straight back, and to our delight said he had found Klara's internment records with a very clear photograph of her taken by MI5.

I went to the Isle of Man for the first time in July of that year and he proved to be so helpful I could not believe my luck. At last, a close up photo of David's mother! He had all sorts of research papers, letters and records ready for me. I made copious notes and when I got home, my first job was to get a good copy of Klara's photograph and frame. It hangs on our wall in a prominent position.

Email from Isle of Man

From: Sims, Roger [roger.sims@mnh.gov.im]
Sent: 09 June 2003 10:16
To: Stern, Christina
Subject: re: Klara Stern

Dear Ms Stern
Thank you for your recent enquiry.
Klara Stern's security registration record here confirms that she arrived in the United Kingdom (Harwich) on New Year's Eve 1938. The registration record also contains a good deal of other information which would I think be useful to you for the purposes of your research.
I am quite prepared to provide access to Klara Stern's record providing that you can confirm that she is infact dead. As you will appreciate Data Protection legislation does not apply to deceased persons.
The Library's data base of internment records contains several separate deposits of recollections and reminiscences of the type which you enquire about. These records are available only in the Library Reading Room and cannot reasonably be copied by the Library staff on behalf of distance enquirers. The best course therefore would be for you to visit here. The Library staff would be only too pleased to give every possible help should you decide to consult these items in person. To this end a printout of these items has been made which can be sent to you on receipt of your postal address.
I should mention also that the Library holds several administrative files for the Rushen Internment Camp, which you should consult also.
I look forward to hearing further from you.
Yours sincerely

Roger M C Sims BA DAA DPESS
Librarian Archivist
Manx National Heritage
Douglas, Isle of Man, IM1 3LY, British Isles
Tel: + 44 (0) 1624 648000
Fax : +44 (0) 1624 648001
E-mail: Roger.Sims@mnh.gov.im
Web site: http://www.gov.im/mnh

WARNING If you are not the intended addressee of this e-mail, you must not copy or deliver it to anyone else or use it in any unauthorised manner.

Now, in 2015, everything has changed, and the jigsaw is almost complete. We have finally accepted that some pieces will always be missing, but I believe this does not spoil the picture. If anything, it adds to it.

David through the years

David, the Boy

There is not a lot to say about the boy David, except that he has very few memories before he was adopted at the age of eight. His adoptive sister did once tell me that he was a very naughty child, and that he would not sit down in the bath! He was also in and out of the water quickly. He remembers being made to practise playing the piano in the cold, so it was no pleasure. He stopped playing as soon as he could. He never felt as though he belonged, and when David's adoptive father died, he made that true from the grave when it said in his Will ' and to my adopted son David, £5,000.' David's adoptive father was a rich man when he died, and his own son and daughter benefitted greatly.

David, the Man

We've been together now for more than forty years, and I love David more now than I did all that time ago. We have had much laughing, living and loving in that time and we have indulged our love of travelling. It was on one such trip to Prague in 2008 that we went to Terezin, (Theriesenstadt, in German.) This is the place where David's grandparents were sent by the Nazi's all those years ago. It was certainly a visit to remember, and one both of us will never forget. It was the last attempt I made at finding out anything further. I left behind us details of David's grand-parents, and our address in England.

Many weeks afterwards, I received a photocopy of a document confirming Adolph's death there, but alas, nothing new. When I got back to England, I was left wanting to know more about Theriesenstadt and the people who were sent there. I borrowed an obscure book by Norbert Troller and it was so good. (I photocopied it, typed it out and have included it for anyone to read.)

We have lived at two more addresses since our time in the cottage, and are now well settled in a bungalow. I still think David does not look his age, when you think he is nearer to 80 than 70!

He resumed piano lessons just this year, and he is thoroughly enjoying them – he's good too. It has become a joke between us that he always prefers a shower to a bath, and he showers at the speed of sound! But I love him today as I did in 1973!

Epilogue

I added some more to this writing recently, it makes me sad today that the world is so full of unrest and many thousands of people are suffering, just like they always have – things change, do they? It is over twenty years since I wrote the piece for David's children, and they were really pleased that they had their history. How easy it seems, that a situation like the one Hitler created, could so easily be re-created. Then all of our family members would be seen as a nuisance and something to be got rid of. It does not bear thinking about, and scares me rigid to say the least. I have not tried to explain the inexplicable, just used facts as I know them, with a little bit of poetic licence – that is, my thoughts.

Further reading and references:

Berghahn, M. (1984) German Jewish Refugees in England – Ambiguities of Assimilation.

Macmillan, London

Blodig V. PhD (2003) Terezin – Places of suffering and braveness. Booklet bought at Terezin ISBN 80-86758-11-7

Burleigh, M. (2000) The Third Reich – a new history. Basingstoke, London

Ceserani, D. and Kushner, T. 1993,

The Internment of Aliens in 20th Century Britain, Frank Cass (2006) in Women's experience of Internment by Marion Koch, p. 147 Manx Heritage Library

Fritta,B. Old people in the attics, Terezin 1943-1944, hand drawing,

Dischner, Fisher, Tashenbuck, Verlag (eds) (1982) Eve Stummer Generation Pp63-69

Ellen,(unpublished) 10th March, 2001 Ellen now lives in Warwick in England

Island of Barbed Wire, (1984) Connery Chapell, Corgi Books

Isle of Man Examiner (1943) – June 7th p. 8

Nicholes, LH, 2002 A Rose in War Part 1 Barbed Wire Granite Publishing USA

Ogbe, H. (2001) The Crumbs of the Wife's Table Spectrum Books, Ibadan, Nigeria
Thomas Fritta-Haas, permanent loan to the Jewish Museum Berlin
Troller. Norbert., (1991) THERESIENSTADT: HITLER'S GIFT TO THE JEWS Copyright © 1991 by the University of North Carolina Press

Useful websites
www.kindertransport.com
www.myjewishlearning.com
www.wikipedia.org/wiki/**Stutthof**_concentration_**camp**

Printed in the United States
By Bookmasters